839.8226
Ib7gm

IBSEN,

...

The Dramaturgy of Fear

MICHAEL GOLDMAN

WITHDRAWI

COLUMBIA UNIVERSITY PRESS

NEW YORK

LIBRARY ST. MARY'S COLLEGE

Columbia University Press
Publishers Since 1893
New York   Chichester, West Sussex

Copyright © 1999 Columbia University Press
All rights reserved

Library of Congress Cataloging-in-Publication Data
Goldman, Michael, 1936–
    Ibsen : the dramaturgy of fear / Michael Goldman.
        p. cm.
    Includes index.
    ISBN 0–231–11320–x. — ISBN 0–231–11321–8 (pbk.)
        1. Ibsen, Henrik, 1828–1906—Criticism and interpretation.
    2. Fear in literature. I. Title.
PT8895.G58 1999
839.2'226—dc21   98–19248

Casebound editions of Columbia University Press books are printed on
permanent and durable acid-free paper.
Printed in the United States of America
c 10 9 8 7 6 5 4 3 2 1
p 10 9 8 7 6 5 4 3 2 1

LIBRARY ST. MARY'S COLLEGE

For Eleanor

CONTENTS

ACKNOWLEDGMENTS

PORTIONS OF THIS BOOK, NOW IN MUCH REVISED FORM, appeared originally in *American Imago* 51, no. 3 (Fall 1994). I am grateful to The Johns Hopkins University Press for permission to use this material. My special thanks go to Louise Kaplan for inviting me to contribute. A residency at the Rockefeller Study Center at Bellagio was both sweet and useful at an early stage.

I am grateful, too, to Maurice Charney for the invitation to speak that started me on the path to this book, and to Michael Cadden, Richard Greenberg, Richard Kuhns, and James Shapiro for encouragement and discussion at propitious times. Joen Bille and Sigrunn Omark were of inestimable help on Norwegian matters.

At Columbia University Press Jennifer Crewe, even among her many responsibilities, has always found time for generous and thoughtful guidance. Rita Bernhard was a sensitive and efficient copy editor.

Finally, my deepest debt is to my wife, Eleanor Bergstein, who has helped and led and delighted and strengthened me through every stage and page of the project. Here as in all things, I have been blessed by her love, intelligence, and humane wisdom.

M.G.
New York
April 1998

IBSEN

CHAPTER ONE

Torpedoing the Ark

IBSEN'S CHARACTERS ARE KILLERS. Even in their staid northern parlors, they maneuver with a cruel and resourceful ferocity. Jean Giraudoux once said that a play by Racine is "a series of negotiations between wild beasts"; his remark seems to work even better for plays like *Ghosts* and *Rosmersholm*. Of course, some talent for inflicting pain—or, to put it more politely, the ability to imagine characters who possess such talent—is basic equipment for any dramatist. Moment to moment, good dramatic dialogue sustains action by compelling a response—one character forcing another to react—and to do anything that *requires* a reaction is to do some kind of hurt, to violate another person's autonomy and thus to leave a scar. Artaud's "Everything that acts is a cruelty" is in this sense simply an elementary principle of drama. But Ibsen's characters are quite extraordinarily gifted at getting their claws in. Active, passive, oblique, direct, with an "involuntary" phrase or a frontal assault, even from beyond the grave they do their damage brilliantly. Rebecca West drives Beata Rosmer and then John Rosmer to suicide, but Rosmer deftly persuades Rebecca to kill herself, too, and poor, sick, victimized Beata turns out to have left behind some cunningly conceived hints and letters that make sure the lovers will be destroyed, especially given her brother Kroll's lesser but still well-developed gift for exploiting human weakness. Even self-effacing Aline Solness manages, in her dim, flustered, "dutiful" way, to get off the verandah in time to ensure that her husband will not be prevented from making his fatal climb at the end of *The Master Builder*. A distinct part of the pleasure in Ibsen is watching these compact thrusts at the jugular strike home.

This savage, bracing destructiveness is something most readers and audiences feel in Ibsen's work as a whole. The plays themselves are killers. The ruthlessness of their vision (in a later chapter we shall see that Ibsen himself associates it with the eyes of an abused and vengeful child) seems directed—though with a tonic clarity and thoroughness—not just at the characters but at the audience. Their spirit seems well expressed in Ibsen's wonderful little poem, "To My Friend, the Revolutionary Orator":

I won't play at moving chessmen.
Knock over the board; then I'm with you.
You furnish the deluge for the world.
I'll gladly torpedo the Ark.

The last phrase is breathtaking. It suggests a sweeping completeness of attack next to which most notions of revolutionary upheaval seem timid or sentimental. To save mankind it is necessary to imagine blowing up anything constructed to save it—no, to imagine it *so that* it blows up. That would be the playwright's gift, to depict the "ark" so thoroughly, so clearly, so unsparingly that it blows up by itself, as when in *Ghosts* Mrs. Alving's play-long drive toward freedom propels her into a horror from which she can never be free. Memorable points about this or that ark, about society or its members, may be made along the way, but above all we respond to the ferocious effectiveness of the explosion. Torpedoing the ark, one might say, is the signature energy of Ibsen's drama, the irony behind the tragedy, the joy behind the irony, the grimness in the amber of the joy.

These observations are attempts to describe an extended *dramatic effect*, a passage of feeling or sensation created by a play as it unfolds. They belong to the type of impression from which our understanding of any dramatist's work must ultimately spring, all sense of its meaning, value, unique contribution. They refer, that is, to a play's immediate impact, its power to move, excite, awaken us, to that initial thump of being, of redirected energy, of altered sight and pulse from which all the secondary elaborations we make as critics and readers must flow. Richard Gilman reminds us that Ibsen's plays, like all plays, are first of all "sensuous objects."[1] To think about Ibsen's dramatic effects is to return to the fact that he is a playwright—that he makes his distinctive claim on us in the first instance through our experience of a dramatic object, through the unfolding textures of performance, through all the topographies and energies of the stage. "Dramatic effect" makes up a broad category, whose boundaries are inevitably blurred, and yet it is of a precision appropriate to the study of Ibsen's art. If we wish to stabilize our responses to the plays in terms of idea, the most valuable ideas we associate with Ibsen will be those that are startled into wakefulness by his effects or that describe or account for their impact, especially as it is felt in the theater.

The examples of dramatic effect to which I have already referred are, to say the least, large and complex; they are constellations of effect built up out of many elements. And since they are cumulative, it is not really possible to separate them surgically from "ideas," from matters of reflection and interpretation. Indeed, the point of thinking about them is to see how reflection and interpretation, how all the movements of thought and emotion that we attach to the plays flow from and through those impacts and surges of response that we call dramatic effects.

The notion of dramatic experience, indeed of experience of any sort, raises all kinds of delectable philosophical questions, of which the most accurate thing to say is that they have not been satisfactorily answered. Such questions need not detain us here. For whatever reason, we are conscious of having the whatever-it-is we call experience, and we know that in the theater it strikes us with a determinative, savorable sharpness. My notion is that we can benefit by keeping that kind of experience before us. It is a matter of usefully focusing one's attention, rather than of rigorous definition.

My hope is that this book will increase our under-standing of Ibsen's power. Certainly Ibsen has long been acknowledged as a major dramatist and a significant intellectual figure (though often with a certain conde-scension, which we will need to explore). But in many respects our sense of the exact texture of his art remains limited, and as a result we have a limited awareness of where his plays are offering to take us. I think much more may be done to observe and examine his dramatic effects and thereby to connect his dramatic practice to its specif-ic cultural force. Of what are these effects composed? How are they notated? How do they summon and structure emotion? What connections do they establish between the virtuosity of actors and the expectations of an audience? How do they make a claim on the modern imagination? The aim is to look more closely at how Ibsen deploys the materials available to him as a playwright to solicit and inflect, construct and reconstruct (at times quite precisely to deconstruct) our response.

These chapters deliberately focus on features of Ibsen's dramaturgy that have been overlooked or underread, and thus they must leave much out of account, but I hope they constitute something like a journey to the center of his dramatic style. They begin as an attempt to characterize that style by looking at theatrical effect and histrionic prac-tice, and then go on to look at what I take to be one of the central vibrations that the style gives off, examining some of the apprehensions of human possibility and history which may grip us when that characteristic "vision" takes hold. Finally I return, as it were, to the surface in order to do justice to some other critically neglected dramatic effects necessary to complete my account, effects this time connected to sensual pleasure and happiness.

Surface and center aren't so easily separated, of course, nor should they be. I hope, however, that this book provides a deeper appreciation of how Ibsen's dramaturgy works. This means looking both at what an Ibsen play feels like as it comes at us, especially in the theater, and at what kind of adjustments in our relation to life it may leave us with. In what follows I concentrate on some main motors of response in Ibsen's theatrical art, in which acting technique, patterns of feeling, visual and verbal imagery, and the choice of situation and character fuse, finally, to produce those sensations I have gestured at in the phrase "torpedoing the ark" and to fill them with content. I hope the approach will prove its value by the light it casts on a wide range of subjects, from Ibsen's contribution to modern acting, to the design of individual plays, to their still urgent cultural implications.

I

I want to begin with a series of moments that recur frequently in Ibsen's plays, especially those of his artistic maturity. These moments are frequent and emphatic enough almost to constitute a kind of dramatic signature themselves, though as far as I know they have not been noticed by criticism. They are moments of sharply specific feeling, both for characters and audiences, and are generally driven home by a distinctive vocabulary, verbal and gestural. They of course illustrate the importance of looking carefully at Ibsen's theatrical notation and its impact, but, even more, they are widely revealing as to his dramaturgy in general.

The passages I have in mind all occur at moments of crisis, usually climactic moments, and they exhibit a striking similarity of gesture and language. For the characters, they are moments of dread, of an overwhelming or uncanny terror which goes well beyond the circumstances that cause it. They are accompanied by a remarkably varied vocabulary of fear, which is dominated by the Dano-Norwegian word *angst* and takes on many of the ethical connotations that term has enjoyed in our culture since Kierkegaard. There are hints of such moments in the early plays—and more than a hint in *Brand*—but the moment appears unmistakably in *Peer Gynt*. There, not surprisingly, its meanings are spelled out with a special fullness.

Peer's voyage home after half a lifetime adventuring abroad ends in shipwreck off the Norwegian coast. Exposed to the waves, clinging to the keel of an upturned boat, he is joined by the Strange Passenger, who asks him:

My friend have you even once a year
Known the true anguish of the soul?[2]

"Anguish of the soul" is *angstens alvor* (II, 211), seriousness of dread, fear, angst.[3] The Stranger is there to insist that the value of dread has been missing in Peer's career of evasion, of going "roundabout." It soon becomes plain that Ibsen puts a great deal of weight on the formula, *angstens alvor*. Peer makes it back to Norway. After a scene in which he tries to peel an onion and becomes agitated when he can find no "heart" beneath its many layers—an emblem of his own lack of a center—Peer, who is by now crawling about on all fours, hears the voice of his devoted Solveig singing, "Come back, come back to me," addressing him, her long-defected husband. He rises, "hushed and deathly pale" and reflects on "One who remembered and one who forgot . . ." (134) At this point, we hear the words *angst* and *alvor* again:

O, alvor!—og aldri kan det lekes om!
O, angst!—*Her* var mitt keiserdom! (II, 219)

To translate literally, "O seriousness—and it can never be played again. / O dread—here was my empire."

Just before what he fears will be his final meeting with the Button Molder, from whom he expects a decision about the fate of his soul, Peer sees a shooting star. He hails it as a brother: "We flash for a moment, then our light is quenched, / And we disappear into the void for ever." Then in the words of the stage direction he "Composes himself as though frightened (*som i angst*)," goes deeper into the mist, and cries out, "Is there no one, no one in all the Universe— / No one in the Abyss—no one in Heaven?" He tears his hair as he realizes he himself is no one, then hears the churchgoers sing and, again following the stage direction, "Crouches in terror (*skrekk*)" and describes himself as dead, what is inside him as waste and desert (*øde*) (154–55; II, 233).

The emotion at issue in all these scenes is not fear of death or of pain, but—as the exchange with the Strange Passenger suggests—the anguish that comes at discovering the need to judge one's life seriously, to hold what Ibsen in a famous poem calls "Doomsday judgment on the soul":

Å *leve* er—krig med trolle
i hjertets og hjernens hvelv.
Å *dikte*,—det er å holde
dommedag over seg selv. (I, 404)

[To live is to battle with trolls
in the vaults of one's heart and brain.
To write is to hold
a doomsday judgment on one's soul.]

Peer discovers that to go straight through instead of roundabout is the course of true freedom and possible salvation, but it's a terrifying choice. The affinities with Kierkegaard are obvious, though Ibsen vehemently denied any influence. This is the metaphysical anguish and sense of loneliness that accompanies an awareness of one's freedom to choose.[4] It is often also accompanied in Ibsen by a sense of waste (*øde*) and/or emptiness (*tomhet*). It is the dark side of Nora's discovery of freedom in *A Doll's House*. Nora's exit from her marriage into a bitter and unfriendly winter night clearly parallels her friend Dr. Rank's departure to face a lonely death, and though Nora does not collapse like Peer, her husband does. As he buries his face in his hands, his word for what he feels is "empty" (*tomt*).[5]

With *Ghosts*, we return more explicitly to the motifs of *Peer Gynt*. The climaxes of the last act are built on a pattern of growing dread, as Mrs. Alving learns the full extent of her son Osvald's syphilitic decline. Like the terminally ill Dr. Rank, Osvald provides a parallel, in physical terms, to the heroine's ethical anguish.

—Now have I taken away all your remorse and self-reproach?
—Yes, you have. But who'll take away the fear (*angsten*)? (270, 153)

Again, the feelings of a man facing death parallel those of a woman facing freedom. The play ends with Mrs. Alving (again following the stage directions carefully) screaming and shrinking back, paralyzed with horror and fright (*redsel*). Ibsen wants to leave us with the sense not simply of a painful dilemma or a pathetic fate but of an uncanny fear.

Also important is the gestural notation Ibsen frequently insists on in these moments. After Brand, near the end of his play, has said that the horror of dreams is over and now comes the horror (*gru*) of life, Gerd, the wild girl he has met on the mountaintop, shrieks with terror (*redsel*), and Brand shrinks (*krymper*) before the avalanche (II, 122–26). Peer crouches (*kryper*) in fright at the Pilgrims' Pentecostal song, Torvald sinks down in a chair before saying "Empty," Osvald "appears to crumple inwardly (*skrumpe*)" (275, 156). Even in *The Wild Duck*, where there is no single figure who can make a genuine movement toward freedom, when Gregers, the prophet of self-liberation, learns of Hedvig's suicide, for which he is responsible, he stands "in a convulsive fit of horror" (*skrekkslagen i krampaktige rykninger*) (489, 277). Again Ibsen specifies a gesture of physical contraction, of shrinking or crumpling or collapse at the moment of dread. And in every case there is the accompanying sense of desolation and emptiness.

Awareness of this motif helps us to notice similar effects even when the gestural delineation is less specific. For instance, it is crucial to be aware of the dread that builds during the last act of *Rosmersholm*. When Rebecca begins to hint darkly at what she may have to do to convince Rosmer of her faith in him, the transaction that quickly leads to their joint suicide, he "start[s] as if in dread [*angst*]" (581, 325). A little earlier he has cried out, "I can't bear this desolation, this awful nothingness [more literally, "terrible emptiness"], this—this—" (577) and the rhythm of the speech in the original suggests the intensity of his fear. "Jeg baerer ikke dette øde, denne forferdelige tomhet,—dette—dette—" (323). Again the character suddenly feels alone with powers that can tear him apart.

"I can't bear it" is a frequent marker of theatrical impact in Ibsen, and its significance should not be overlooked. Today I suspect that readers and actors tend to pass this phrase by with some embarrassment, seeing in it a trace of Victorian grandiloquence, the kind of melodramatic residue which criticism has been all too eager to detect in Ibsen. In fact, as its link to Ibsen's lexicon of fear indicates, it should alert us to an upheaval in a character's psychological career, the eruption of forces that can no longer be contained or denied.

From *Rosmersholm* on, the source of dread we have been tracing grows more explicitly sexual and internal. In *Hedda Gabler*, even though there is no moment exactly of the type I have been describing, it again helps to be aware of the model. The situation is similar to that in *The Wild Duck*. There is no character whom we are allowed to see making a sweeping movement toward freedom and thus toward the dread that comes with confronting it. Hedda's own fears confine her to trying to act through others. But Hedda herself is a source of dread. Her command over the people around her is something like the appeal of the Stranger in *Lady from the Sea*—an attractive and destructive power related to suppressed impulses, to sources we might today call "unconscious," and that in Ibsen are often figured by natural forces of destruction—fire, avalanche, the mill race. Hedda is herself a victim of buried impulses, but we feel the dreadfulness of her power—especially in the great scene when she burns Løvborg's manuscript—and other characters respond to her with fear and crumpling. Later, when she tells her husband Tesman what she has done, his reaction is a "start of terror (*skrekk*)" (766, 427). Her suicide leaves Judge Brack "in [his] armchair, prostrated."

II

The gestural/emotive vocabulary I have been describing largely disappears after *Hedda*, where, as we have seen, it is already muted or dispersed. But the fear remains, its source in the later plays more clearly internalized, a destructive energy inseparable from buried impulses, from unexpressed or unconscious desires. An especially close examination of this kind of fear and its role in human affairs may be found in *The Master Builder*, where the terror of the play's conclusion is apparently the result of external events but actually gains its force by compelling us to participate in impulses we have learned over the course of the play to experience as internal to the hero's mind.

"Projection," in the modern psychological sense, is one of the play's basic mechanisms, both in the characters' relations with one another and on at least one crucial occasion in our relation to what is happening on stage. I am thinking of Hilda's first entrance, one of Ibsen's most daring stage effects. In the dialogue leading up to it, Solness, the successful local builder, has been raising questions for us about certain peculiar mental powers he claims to possess. We have already seen that he exercises some kind of mind control over his secretary, Kaja. The young woman's infatuation seems disturbingly extreme, and the middle aged Solness manipulates it with an equally disturbing intensity. Is he using sex appeal or hypnotizing her? Discussing his powers with Dr. Herdal, he attributes them to a type of telepathy, and we in the audience are uncertain how to judge his claims. Will this play allow us to do what theater audiences are always eager to do, that is, indulge a hankering for the supernatural, the mysterious, the magical? Or are we being given evidence of an aberration? Our uncertainty is heightened when Solness goes on to demand of Herdal whether his wife has asked the Doctor to investigate Solness's mental stability. Now we are forced to wonder: Has Solness guessed something? Is he crazy to suspect? Or is it a bit of both—is he crazy *and* right to suspect that they think he's crazy? Is he preternaturally alert to the activities of those around him or is he "projecting?" And how do his suspicions affect our understanding of his telepathic/mystical claims? In any case, to sum up, Ibsen has maneuvered our reactions to the point where we now have a heightened, somewhat eager awareness of possibly unusual mental powers and of questionable currents of mental suggestion, reinforced by our aesthetic doubts about how to read the signals we are receiving. Solness proceeds to heighten further our sense of an uncertain mixture of slight paranoia and hypernormal alertness (both in the character and ourselves) by talking about his fears:

SOLNESS: It racks me, this fear—it racks me, morning and night. Because someday things have to change, you'll see.

HERDAL: Oh, rot! Where's this change coming from?

SOLNESS: From the young. . . . The change is coming. I can sense it. And I feel that it's coming closer. Some one or other will set up the cry: Step back for *me*! And all the others will storm in after, shaking their fists and shouting: make room—make room—make room! Yes, Doctor, you better look out. Someday youth will come here, knocking at the door—

HERDAL: (*laughing*): Well, good Lord, what if they do?

SOLNESS: What if they do? Well, then it's the end of
   Solness, the master builder.
(A knock at the door to the left) (799–800)

The visitor will turn out to be Hilda Wangel, young and
insistent, whose romantic focus on Solness will unsettle and
excite him and eventually spur him to his death, when she
urges him to climb the tower he has built atop his new
house, in spite of his fear of heights. But at this moment,
before we meet her, the dramatic point is simply that Solness has made a prediction and, uncannily, it has been
fulfilled—as if by thinking it, he has made it happen. Our
own curiosity, doubt, and eagerness have helped prepare
the moment. With one part of our mind, no doubt, we are
ready, like Herdal, to offer a rational explanation, but there
is also the frisson, the uncanniness, the theatrical thrill, that
comes from suddenly getting what we have irrationally,
perhaps guiltily, desired. For us, for the moment, it's *as if*
Solness's thoughts had materialized.

Our response at this point involves an unusually direct
experience of psychic material central to the play. It will be
recalled that Freud accounts for the uncanniness of moments like Hilda's knock on the door by explaining that
they arouse our fear of what he calls "the omnipotence of
thoughts," the primitive belief that mental activity, especially unspoken desires, can of itself have physical consequences. Fear of the omnipotence of thoughts is deeply
embedded in *The Master Builder*.

To understand the weight Ibsen gives to this psychic

material, it will be useful to look for what actors trained in the Stanislavsky method would call the "spine" of the play. A spine is a formula that attempts to express the unified movement of purpose that presumably informs a play, some common thrust underlying the projects or dominant motivations of its characters. A spine must always be cast in the form of an infinitive phrase, as in the spine Francis Fergusson suggests for *Ghosts*, "To control the Alving heritage for my own life" or Harold Clurman's spine for *Heartbreak House*, "To get the Hell out of this place."[6] The infinitive guarantees that what is described will be action, purposive movement, a dynamic experiential texture rather than a theme or idea. As such, it is helpful not only to critics but to directors and actors trying to focus a performance. For reasons that will become clear, it is a technique especially relevant to Ibsen.

The best spine I can find for *The Master Builder* comes from a phrase of Hilda's; it is *to climb as high as you build*, in the sense of to do what you imagine, to act out what you desire, to make happen what you will. This can be seen of course everywhere in Solness's part, not only in his ill-fated effort on the tower but in such actions as imposing his will on Kaja or creating his first houses after the fire. But it also applies to Hilda's whole project with Solness in which she works to make her fantasy come true, to the aspiring young architect Ragnar Brovik's wish to build what he's designed, to his father Knut's wish to see his boy successful, and even, I would say, to Aline Solness's insistence on acting according to the principle of duty she has lived by. The most incendiary example is the one Hilda urges on Solness—to have the forbidden sexual object you desire.

Hilda's scariness for Solness is not only that she forces him to acknowledge that he sexually molested her as a child and to reenact the other chief occurrence of that day—his climbing the tower in spite of his fear of heights. It is that Hilda in so many ways seems to embody Solness's own thoughts—as for instance when she persuades him to place his imprimatur on Ragnar's drawings, saying "You've got to" and "Oh, how I hate this [Ragnar]" and "Nobody but you should have a right to build" (821, 834, 836). Her statements may be contradictory, but they accurately represent Solness's conflicting feelings.

These mental phenomena are given a large setting by the story of the fire that destroyed Aline Solness's family home. Solness was in no way responsible for the fire, but he had wished for it, had imagined it happening, because it would put him in business as a builder. After the disaster, by building homes on the ruins and in the garden of the old house, he first made his professional mark. Since then, both he and his wife have felt profound guilt, and their married life has been joyless. This is a myth about the omnipotence of thoughts as a founding principle of civilization, or rather about the founding of civilization on the basis of desires whose destructive component, turned inward, persists as guilt. The story of Solness's success as an architect—the transformation of the inherited garden through wished-for violence into a scene of building and anxiety—is the same one Freud was to tell in *Civilization and Its Discontents*.

The high point of terror in *The Master Builder* comes at the play's climax, when Solness's body is seen hurtling to the ground. We only glimpse the body from a great distance as it falls, so, as I have said, we may consider this a very externalized moment, but the pattern I have been tracing allows us to see the moment in a different light—and to appreciate its theatrical effectiveness in urgently involving us in the conflict of internal, psychological forces.

Though Solness is offstage when he mounts the tower, it's as if the buried impulses active in his mind take over the stage as he climbs, battling it out till at their peak of frenzy he falls and dies. I do not mean this at all allegorically but rather as a felt participation, from the inside, as it were, in the eruption of his buried desire into act. Each of the three main characters onstage as he climbs seems to embody one of the forces we have already seen at work in Solness's imagination. Aline, with her agitated insistence that he must not do it, reflects his guilt; Hilda, who eggs him on, his desire; Ragnar, who keeps saying it is impossible, that Solness cannot take a step further, his fear. And, as if to heighten our sense that it is the very conflict among these impulses that kills him, we have Doctor Herdal desperately begging them all to be quiet. We are plunged into Solness's own terrified experience of the attempt to climb as high as he has built.

Nor should we forget the impression young Ragnar makes at the end. Here the familiar gesture of collapsing with terror reemerges in a little-noticed passage that repeats the basic process of the play. Ragnar has been full of hostility toward Solness, has said that Solness cannot climb the tower, is sure to fall; he has been longing to replace him. Now suddenly Solness is killed, and Ragnar is literally paralyzed with fright—"I can't move," he says (859). He leans trembling against the railing and can barely speak. The Master Builder is dead and the new Master Builder is filled with horror because his desires have been realized. Ragnar's life is repeating Solness's. The cycle of guilt that started with the fire has begun again.[7]

III

Though these moments of fear become more explicitly internal in origin as we go through the great sequence of prose plays, even from the first there is an emphasis on inwardness in exploring them, on impulses that only emerge after following complicated subterranean routes. Especially in passages of great intensity, Ibsen's characters are propelled by emotions that rise from oblique or hidden sources, sources remote from their clear understanding or articulation. For this reason it is revealing to relate Ibsen's emphasis on passages of intense fear to the role of his plays in the development of modern acting style.

Ibsen's scripts, certainly from *A Doll's House* on, charge the actor with manifesting buried, often contradictory drives at moments of crisis. However close they may lie to the surface of the action, these drives are always in some sense alienated from the character, either not fully available to the person who is driven by them or not fully possessed. Nora, at the beginning of *A Doll's House*, stands in no clearly comprehending relation to her childhood, her father, the story of her marriage, the problems of the loan to which she has signed her father's name, and the years of secret copying to pay it off. Though she has some awareness of their role in her life, they drive her in ways she does not understand. This is even more evident in later heroes like Rebecca West or Hedda Gabler or Alfred Allmers.

Just as important, the buried drives are linked to traumatic moments or conditions in the character's past. To achieve authentic feeling in performance, the actor or actress must possess and assemble clues from a character's life that are scattered throughout the text, and draw on them for the energies that move the character through the play. The performer cannot, however, simply assemble and convey them narratively, as a messenger conveys past events in a Greek play, say, or as any number of Shakespearean heroes do as they start out on their projects. Nor, on the other hand, can they directly possess and project the forces that drive them. The audience must feel the gap, the distance, the alienation. Both the drives and their sources in the past must remain to some extent buried, removed, unpossessed, oblique to the text—though they may finally break through in geyserlike eruptions like Hedda's burning of Løvborg's manuscript.

Here, of course, we recognize the dynamics of what was to become the Stanislavskian "subtext." Stanislavsky, we should remember, produced his great codification in response to a psychological crisis in his own career, when he began, quite desperately, to seek an authenticity suitable to the conditions of modern performance. He found it in the currents of unstated, usually no more than half-conscious intention and reminiscence that run beneath a script's surface. Vivid, effective performance depended on allowing these buried currents obliquely but constantly to illuminate the action. It was of course a method deeply suited to the requirements of Ibsen's drama. Still, it should be noted that Ibsen's innovations have implications well beyond Stanislavskian naturalism. Indeed the fundamental situation of a buried or hidden layer of reality from which the character is in some sense alienated, and of a performance style in which the actor gains authenticity by leaping the alienating gap, applies not only to naturalistic acting but to the two other dominant styles of twentieth-century performance, the Brechtian and Artaudian systems, as well.[8] Ibsen is thus in an important sense the inventor of modern acting in general.

But it is also important to recognize that all subtexts are not alike, especially not all naturalistic subtexts. Our familiarity with method acting may blind us not only to Ibsen's historical importance but to the specific texture of the acting he demands. Though Stanislavsky's formulation describes with a certain accuracy a subtext common to all naturalistic drama, the Ibsen subtext is distinctive. It is worth distinguishing, for example, from Chekhov's subtext.

Subtext in Ibsen typically differs from Chekhov in its treatment of what Stanislavsky would call "objectives and superobjectives." An objective, for Stanislavsky, is a character's immediate goal at a particular moment in a scene. Larger goals, toward which the local objectives tend over the course of a play, are called superobjectives. Like spines, objectives and superobjectives lend themselves to description by infinitive phrases. Indeed, any spine attempts, ideally, to be true to all the superobjectives of all the parts of a given play. Now, the objectives one encounters at almost any point in Ibsen's realistic plays are ones of intense, if not always fully conscious will, of propulsive, emphatic purposiveness. They are distinguished by fierce concentration on the superobjective. In studying Ibsen's major roles, one finds that the character's intention at any specific moment will typically come close to the character's large general project. Nora's superobjective—let us describe it as *to free herself of the limitations that encumber her marriage*—is vigorously present in her apparently inconsequential opening line, "Hide the tree!" as she prepares for what she believes will be her first Christmas with Helmer free of financial anxiety. She is urgent that the tree remain a surprise for the children, because she wants this year's celebration to be perfect.

I do not mean that the Ibsen actor should not play local objectives. Nora must concentrate for a beat on focusing the maid's attention and next on getting the tree quickly out of sight. Nevertheless (a) there is almost always an intense focus on *accomplishing* something that hums within an Ibsen character's lines—on making a practical change in the world of the play; and (b) this change is substantial, of a certain magnitude, in the sense that the local objective is likely to be a step in a project to bring about a major re-alignment in the state of affairs, a change that comes close to or points emphatically toward the superobjective.

Clearly this is different from the typical objectives of Chekhov's characters, which are particularly suited to acting classes, since they reproduce the play of velleities and avoidances which give the activities of ordinary life that continual small oblique movement so hard and important to reproduce on stage. When Uncle Vanya makes his first entrance, he says, "Yes . . . Yes . . .," and the subtext is perhaps something like "to forestall the criticism of Astrov and Marina by indicating I'm aware I've been napping at an odd hour, to excuse, to explain." Can one think of any major Ibsen character entering like that? Even if we take a big Chekhov scene, for instance Astrov and Helen in *Vanya*'s third act, the subtext is full of doubts, small wishes, exculpations, regrets. Perhaps Natasha in *The Three Sisters* has a focus as fierce, say, as the maid Regina in *Ghosts*, but who else in her play has? For Chekhov even an active, successful man of affairs like Lopakhin is driven by desires that have only the most remote connection to his practical accomplishments. He goes about his business while his feelings slide in other directions. On stage, the moments when he pursues an agenda are brief and ineffective. By contrast, even something as neutral as Nora's "Hide the tree" must be full of a determination to get things done, an energy tied to years of secret toil and narrow circumstances. And it is the energy of a great, though imperfectly understood project. Ibsen brings Nora on, as he brings on Mrs. Alving and

Rebecca West, on the verge of a great underground achievement. Like them, she will be driven much further than she expects, and, unlike them, she at first thinks her project assimilable to a conventional dream. But the breathless eagerness with which she gives her orders to the maid lies on a vector that runs from the desire to speak obscenities, which she has felt while working to pay off Krogstad's loan, to her wish, later in the play, that she could "tear [her]self to bits," and finally to her break with Torvald.

Thus two features distinguish the Ibsen subtext: big drives and buried drives, projects of liberation from whatever in all those past sources conspires to make liberation terrifying. The point of contrasting Ibsen with Chekhov is to emphasize the intensity, the insistence of that which is repressed. Now, Peer Gynt may seem a great exception here, but he is in fact a revealing variation. Fleeing his home, his marriage, his country, taking to heart the mysterious Boyg's advice to "go roundabout," he seems everywhere to substitute local objectives for any superobjective as a matter of principle. He wants to avoid a showdown at all costs. But his insistence on going roundabout becomes for him a superobjective in itself, a creative avoidance of commitment as passionate, and ultimately as self-terrifying as Brand's pursuit of commitment *tout court*. It is only in act 5, when he is forced to acknowledge this superobjective, that he experiences his first moment of serious dread, of *angstens alvor*.

From this point of view, it is possible to see that *Peer Gynt* is shaped by a series of moments of fear that interrupt its expansive and exotic narrative. And in a development that will become a trademark of the plays Ibsen goes on to write, Peer's earlier moments of fear, apparently quite serious when we first encounter them, give way to deeper difficulties, much less easy to evade. The fairy-tale scariness of the Troll Kingdom and the encounter with the Boyg, even the more extreme grotesquery of the madhouse, pale eventually before the real seriousness of the final act. We will see that sequences of this kind, in which apparent obstacles are replaced by more intransigent, more painfully ethical ones, regularly inform Ibsen's use of "well-made" plot construction in the realistic plays.

As Peer's pattern of pursuit and avoidance, fear and escape intensifies, it is accompanied by a related motif of remembering and forgetting. The motif has a suggestive bearing on Ibsen's relation with modern acting and indeed with modernity in general. It will be recalled that when Peer, finally in the grip of "serious dread," hears Solveig singing in act 5 and cries out, he refers to "One who remembered and one who forgot." Now, of course, a certain kind of forgetting has been a principle of Peer's life, just as a certain kind of alienated remembering has been. (Peer keeps remembering events from his past—but as if they were quotations from scripture or wisdom literature that he has forgotten.) But the suggestive point is that a paradoxical mingling of remembering and forgetting is also a principle of modern naturalistic performance. Naturalistic actors must not only remember a past that their characters have forgotten, they must authentically forget it as well, so that the remembering can struggle with and surprise their forgetting. In Ibsen, a character's conscious will regularly coincides with desires, often unconscious, both to suppress and reactivate the past. The distinctive modernity of this process is suggested by the way it recalls de Man's notion of modernity as a forgetting of the past regularly compelled to remember it;[9] one need only think of Mrs. Alving, Rebecca West, or Solness. In de Man's sense, Ibsen is peculiarly the dramatist of the modern, of the effort to be free in a certain self-undermining way. As de Man points out, this means freedom from the past in all its forms—from institutions, traditions, routines, personal history, indeed from history itself. It is a freedom fundamentally compromised by the very notion of the modern subject, whose subjectivity is inseparable from contradiction.[10]

According to Nietzsche, in order "to achieve something truly new, powerful, life-giving, and original," in order, in short, to be modern, one must overcome history by going back into history to do battle with it—to reopen, confront, reconfigure the past. Only by remembering can we forget. This is a program we find in modern thinkers and artists from Marx to T. S. Eliot. It is certainly the program of Freud and method acting. And while the motif of remembering and forgetting has broad resonances for Ibsen as a modernist, to which we shall return, the crucial dramaturgical issue here can be most clearly stated in psychological terms. The performer of all the great Ibsen roles must marshal the power of the strong drives that make up the alienated subtext, the power of what the audience must experience as "forgotten" wishes—desires suppressed, repressed, censored, or denied. Ibsen's writing stresses the intense and potentially dangerous psychic release of making such desires erupt through the text, in acting out what one usually does not even acknowledge, in climbing as high as one builds.

IV

The terror and anxiety that befall most of Ibsen's main characters are thus connected to the basic anxiety of acting itself, an anxiety that manifests itself most commonly in stage fright. Psychoanalytic studies of stage fright emphasize the degree to which anxiety is created by any acting out of normally suppressed impulses in public. The actor must climb as high as the playwright builds, or as Stephen Aaron puts it, "In the theater the artist 'acts out' in public what the writer, for example, 'thinks out' in private."[11] But the actor is particularly subject to fear in that he must draw on suppressed impulses of his own to make the performance convincing.

What is of preeminent interest here is that the defining characteristics of Ibsen acting unavoidably heighten several elements of performance that are major contributors to stage fright. The first of these is *aggression*. In stage fright the aggressive designs of actor on audience are projected in a fear that the audience is hostile to the actor. If Ibsen's characters tend to be killers peculiarly gifted in finding out and attacking their colleagues' weak points, Ibsen's actors must be able to call upon their own strong aggressive drives, their power to destroy or at least dominate those around them. The trait is reflected in Ibsen's own thoroughgoing destructive temperament as a playwright—his willingness to torpedo the ark.

The second element is fear of punishment for *acting out forbidden desires*. Dramatic characters have always acted out forbidden desires; this is the natural subject for acting, which is after all a form of behavior based on transgressing the usual limits of presented identity as well as on making public what is normally private. In Ibsen, however, to an extent scarcely paralleled in any playwright before him, the requirement is that the actor appear to engage such desires as *buried*—that he project them as pressing from an inner source from which the character is separated.

Finally, there is the *loss of poise-creating mechanisms*. In an important article, Donald Kaplan calls attention to the way theatrical performance prohibits those physical procedures by which we normally achieve poise when appearing in public, such as gestures of hand-to-mouth (like drinking or smoking) or leaning on furniture.[12] Appearing in a play, we are limited only to the gestures our part allows. Clearly by specifying certain behaviors, all dramatic scripts interdict others that might sustain poise, but I do not think it has been observed that the invention of modern naturalistic acting programatically removes a whole battery of such mechanisms. It does this by introducing the alienated subtext, a new set of wholly internal stresses to which the character must be seen to respond. Tom Robertson doesn't demand this kind of acting any more than Scribe. But Ibsen does, and after him Strindberg and Chekhov, though in different ways.

True, in any kind of performance, modern or ancient, the life inside the actor must be felt as in some sense operating below the surface of his script. He must hold on to invisible, ungraspable things—memories, the past, unapprehended intentions. However, to have, like Hamlet, a real, external Ghost to react to gives you an opportunity for poise, a place—à la Garrick—to put the hands, something to push against.[13] But if instead the ghost is a personal history or a system of desires that you only half understand, have half forgotten, want to, need to forget, then a whole layer of stability normally available to defend against the threatening, devouring theater audience is taken away from you. It may be no accident that when, at the height of his career, Laurence Olivier experienced a uniquely violent attack of stage fright, which persisted in a form intense enough nearly to incapacitate him as an actor for five years, the part he was playing was *The Master Builder*.[14]

Indeed a kind of stage fright played a striking part in Ibsen's life while he was composing *Peer Gynt*. During that period he seemed convinced that he would meet a sudden end and was inordinately apprehensive of the dangers of earthquakes, cholera, falling roof slates, savage dogs, and so on. This is perhaps not so surprising in an author who is suddenly coming into his own and fears he will not live to finish a great work. Ibsen had broken through with

Brand, and was writing with a freedom and fluency he had never achieved before. But the fact is that the subject matter of *Peer Gynt* reproduces the very dynamic that links stage fright to the acting of naturalistic drama. And it does so in a way that is suggestive not only for Ibsen but for the activity of the playwright in general—the peculiar negotiation this type of writer is forced to make with that which is not writing.

For what does the pen of a playwright do but produce a writing that enables acting, a kind of writing, that is, that to an unusual degree allows a performer to generate something other than a text? What the actor provides is available only through performance and hence is not reducible to another text. (Acting is not simply a matter of underlining key words, selecting gestures from a conventional alphabet, or adding, as it were, emotional adverbs in parenthesis. We may call what the actor supplies "subtext," but if it were simply another kind of text, another kind of writing, it could be written, and we would not need to go to the theater for it.)[15] Nonetheless it is the gift of the talented dramatist to make acting of a certain excellence possible. It is the playwright's writing that unleashes the action, enables the actor to unleash the transgressive energy, the aggression that makes him an ambivalent cynosure for an audience, a figure of power and danger.

From this standpoint we can see the Ibsen of the 1860s in a new light. He finds himself suddenly releasing new energies in a till now stalled and unsatisfactory career as a playwright, and he does so by writing two plays, *Brand* and

Peer Gynt, that are not plays. He has not yet developed the alienated subtext of modern drama; nevertheless a whole system of alienations, suppressions, and revelations infuses his subject and his attempts to evoke it. He both remembers and forgets the stage. Thus he frees himself for making new demands on actors—and new assaults on the theater audience—by first distancing himself from the problems and practices of acting. He unleashes his own transgressive energies in a play about a supreme liar, a monster of self-indulgence who keeps getting away with it while regularly being threatened with fearful punishments. In some ways the play resembles Shakespeare's *Love's Labor's Lost*, which, like *Peer Gynt*, is both a supreme example of an author's newly burgeoning poetic gift and a searching criticism of that gift's limitations and dangers. Where Shakespeare concentrates on the problematics of language, however, *Peer Gynt* focuses on the imagination's metamorphic power. The play makes poetic use of the dizzying, half-fearful excitement that can accompany any triumphant exercise of the imagination (as when a child discovers he can get away with lying). It reflects Ibsen's sense of his new high-flying powers and yet, with that kind of doomsday intensity of self-judgment manifested for the first time in *Brand*, it sees the dangers of the life of the imagination, the self-indulgence, the vanity, the hysteria, the loss of self in selfishness and in the pathways of self-contemplation. Beyond this, there is also a sense of the terrible psychic energies let loose by giving free rein to the imagination, energies that come home to punish their possessor.

The play is filled with terrifying images of mutilation and deformity, including the boy who chops off his finger to escape the draft, the troll child, and the threatened operation on Peer's eyes. One reason we side with Peer is that he doesn't want to be mutilated. He wants to live out a freedom equal to his happiest feelings, to the yeasty vitality we appreciate at the play's beginning and which is the source of his exuberant imagination. In this, he exerts something like the appeal of Hal in his Falstaff mode. (This is not the appeal of Falstaff himself; Peer is not a Falstaff. But he lives in the way that life with Falstaff may tempt Hal to live. Indeed *Peer Gynt* may help us to understand better the joy and centrality of Falstaff's lying.)

The prodigal breakneck energy and grotesque imagery of the play suggest how high the stakes are for its writer. We experience *Peer Gynt* in part as a flight from mutilation into some longed-for preservation of the total self. This experience can be compared to certain questions. How can imagination in its most vital, its freest form, keep free, without becoming merely an evasion, a self-indulgence? How can imagination's natural impulse to roundaboutness, escape, fantasy, shape-changing, animal delight, pure asocial assertion, violence, even madness, win through without corrupting or destroying its possessor? The play's pattern of mutilations reaches its climax in a scene in a madhouse where a man who imagines he has been *turned into a pen* calls out to Peer to use him, and then, in order to sharpen himself, cuts his own throat. At this point Peer sinks to the floor screaming for help and is derisively crowned King of the Self by his fellow inmates. It is a nightmare image of writing as self-realization as self-destruction. Little wonder that Ibsen experienced such surges of fear during *Peer Gynt*'s composition. In order not to be afraid of writing, he had to become afraid of almost everything else.

V

The sense of risk that so deeply informs *Peer Gynt* is thus more than casually related to the psychology of stage fright and its connection to naturalistic acting. In *Peer Gynt* the risk is a projection of the writer's terrifying exercise of his imagination, a force that is at once self-defining and self-lacerating. *Peer Gynt* everywhere suggests—in its plot, topography, imagery, even in the movements of its characters—that the project of self-realization is not only bewildering, confusing, contradictory, and roundabout but is radically frightening as well. Not the least of its terrors is that what most frightens you may turn out to be yourself—yourself as troll or Boyg or manic writing instrument. And even more terrifying is that these crises of self-dread reflect the self as empty. In the realistic plays, the risk and terror become associated with characters whose projection in the theater requires the new lability demanded by modern acting, with the presence of performers who must themselves project a dangerous buried life.

From this vantage point the recurrent gesture of crumpling to which I referred at the beginning of the chapter, the shrinking and collapsing that occur at the moment of dread, can now be seen as a historically potent revision of a basic histrionic gesture, one very common in the iconography of acting. I mean that it resembles, yet in a way is the opposite of, a familiar posture of possession, a physical sign by means of which the actor is seen to be possessed by emotion and to possess the stage. From the cavorting of the New Guinea *samhuna* to Garrick seeing old Hamlet's ghost, from the teapot stance to the antics of the Duke and the Dauphin, acting and pictorial representations of acting have always focused on postures which in their tension and exaggerated projection outward have reflected the uncanny liberation, the emotional plangency and release of acting.

At least until the nineteenth century, this familiar gesture also suggested possession by spirits. The actor typically looked like someone who had seen a ghost, which his character often had. Indeed the transfer of supernatural energies from one figure to another, like the contagiousness of the plague in Artaud, is too apt a description of the basic processes of dramatic performance to be simply a metaphor. "Nothing," as T. S. Eliot remarks, "is more dramatic than a ghost."[16] Our idea of "haunting" closely approximates the instigating action of drama, whatever goads a character, actorlike, to abandon the limits of normal behavior and *act* in both senses of the term. However stylized the performance, an actor takes on the life of another as if it were a ghostly command.

But though Ibsen's crumpling gesture may remind us of this motif—though it may seem at first glance to be yet another version of the emotive stances typical of acting in any period—it is crucially different. If anything, it looks like the inverse of the Garrickian gesture, implosion rather than explosion. But while superficially it may suggest being crushed from the outside, we have seen that what makes the characters crumple is the surprising and disturbing nature of what is going on inside them. And though it sometimes, as in *Brand* and *Peer Gynt*, occurs in response to supernatural voices, it always suggests that the force is less possessive than evacuative. The posture, inescapably, suggests defecation. It is accompanied by waste and emptiness and enfeeblement, by fear and trembling, and its terrifying impulse surges from within—though it surges from an alienated source, a center remote from the character's control and understanding. I have elsewhere pointed out that in the history of drama, when characters are no longer troubled by literal ghosts, they begin to be haunted by memories; perhaps this recurrent gesture in Ibsen reflects the new psychic burdens, the new kind of haunting from within required of the modern actor. In any case, Ibsen's greatest theater texts require that the actor project an inner life that threatens to evacuate, expose, paralyze both performer and character. In the next chapter we shall see that the links we have been exploring between fear and acting in Ibsen point us toward a clearer understanding of what, not very helpfully, we usually refer to as Ibsen's "realistic" style.

CHAPTER TWO

Alienated Subtext and "Realistic" Style

TO CONNECT FEAR AND ACTING in Ibsen is to take a step toward clarifying a still much misunderstood subject—Ibsen's distinctive dramatic style, the style developed in the great sequence of prose plays. For fear is not only an important ingredient of Ibsen's dramatic imagery and of the texture of performance his most important work demands; it relates to the entire ordonnance of his plays. Ultimately it is through the management of plot, incident, and dialogue that the haunting, anxiety-inducing forces I have been describing get transmitted to the actor/characters. Indeed the distinctive gesture of crumpling itself directs us to a defining feature of Ibsen's style, namely, that it is one of constriction, of constraint, and thus, in the root sense, of anxiety.[1]

The lingering notion that there is something transparent or photographic about Ibsen's "realism" can still blind us to the rigors of his style. In terms of its externals, Ibsen's realistic style is a fusion of three elements—a continuous literalism of physical representation; a rigorous method of plotting derived from but not limited to Scribean mechanics; and a regular reference to pressing social issues. Moreover, it is everywhere marked by the now familiar multiple requirements under which every line of dialogue in naturalistic drama must operate, that it must advance the plot, reveal character, be limited to expressions a character might be expected to use in the given circumstances, and so on. Finally it tends, especially at points of crisis, to a heightened psychological velocity; exchanges follow a rigorously credible emotional progression but at an accelerated pace. What all these elements have in common is their contribution to an atmosphere of constraint. The realistic setting, as is typical with realism from *Madame Bovary* on, is invariably presented as a source of confinement, limitation, failure. Social issues are generally figured through the strong negative pressures of society. Most important, the plotting links moment to moment as part of a tightly forged, intricate causal chain. The cumulative effect of the plot, with its unremitting connection of incident with incident, of present with past, of inner life with inner life, reinforced by the emotional velocity and with a regular diet of assaults on the audience's expectations and opinions, is to create a situation that seems to crowd in on the main characters with overwhelming force. And this external rigor everywhere affects the performance style, the subtextual life of the actors.

We must be careful to give performance its due in thinking about style here. It is all too easy to attribute these effects to story or situation, to what is represented rather than how the play attacks us in the theater. The sense of constraint does not come about simply because Ibsen's characters find or feel themselves trapped as the play reaches its climax. It is much more a question of how Ibsen's actors are constrained to perform this discovery, and it is part of a principle that operates not just at the climaxes but throughout the drama.

To appreciate this, however, we must not forget how thoroughly *dramatic* Ibsen's method is. It focuses our excited attention on the dynamics of the present moment. The neat interlinking of incident and information from the past that Ibsen developed from the well-made play may too easily be misread as a kind of novelistic narration. (It is, for example, construed in this fashion by Peter Szondi who, in a still influential study, finds Ibsen's dramaturgy flawed by his recourse to material which, he claims, can only properly be dealt with in a novel.)[2] In performance, however, an Ibsen play strikes us not as a retrospective description of past events but as an unfolding succession of conflicts. Its dialogue constitutes a series of mini-crises that force bits and pieces of the past, with their attendant fears and desires, to be discovered, suffered, defined by the actor/character in the present. The emphasis is on the rendering of spontaneous choice in continually emergent situations. (Thus Stanislavsky's *theory* of character, with its psychological and social determinism, is in fact, as William Worthen suggests, much less appropriate to modern drama than Sartre's existential view.[3] Stanislavsky's explanation of human behavior takes the form of an inexorable working out of fixed motivations in determining environments, but his *practice* is more suited to the kind of drama of which Ibsen is a model.)

The virtuosity of Ibsen's plotting makes it all too easy to read his plays as mystery stories about the past, punctuated by debates and emotional outbursts in the present. Read this way, the latter, of course, are likely to be seen as undramatic or melodramatic. But the drama comes from the way the style of constriction keeps pressing these forgotten forces and sources to leap into the light. Ibsen's characters, like the terminally ill Dr. Rank in *A Doll's House*, are compelled, moment by moment, to carry out experiments on themselves and to adjust to the dismaying results. The feeling for stylistic pressure may help explain Ibsen's fondness for the *folie à deux,* for scenes in which two characters' deep instabilities so mesh that they push each other to madness, suicide, fatal risk. Each presses the psychic trigger in the other.

Increasingly in the realistic plays Ibsen becomes interested in scenes where the crucial source of pressure in the dialogue is subtextual *on both sides.* The technique reaches maturity in *The Wild Duck*, which marks a distinct expansion of the modern theatrical subtext. The three scenes between Gregers and and his half-sister Hedvig are crucial to the play, and require a new kind of interaction of buried currents of feeling if the play is to make sense and prove persuasive.

Hedvig kills herself only because she has first been persuaded by Gregers, much against her inclination, to kill her beloved pet, the wild duck of the title, as a symbolic sacrifice to regain her father's love. In this frame of mind, she seems to lose touch with reality. Her journey to suicide has to be convincing, and it depends on Gregers' being able to reach an isolated, introspective teenager on the threshold of sexuality at her most private depth of fantasy. One reason Gregers can do this is that he instinctively shares her fantasy world; he literally talks her language:

HEDVIG: There's no one who knows [the wild duck], and no one who knows where she's come from, either.

GREGERS: And actually, she's been in the depths of the sea.

HEDVIG: (*glances at him, suppresses a smile, and asks*): Why did you say "depths of the sea"?

GREGERS: What else should I say?

HEDVIG: You could have said "bottom of the sea"—or "the ocean's bottom"?

GREGERS: But couldn't I just as well say "depths of the sea"?

HEDVIG: Sure. But to me it sounds so strange when some one else says "depths of the sea."

GREGERS: But why? Tell me why? . . . Tell me why you smiled.

HEDVIG: That was because always, when all of a sudden— in a flash—I happen to think of that in there, it always seems to me that the whole room and everything in it is called "the depths of the sea." (438)

Gregers understands how Hedvig's mind works because, like her, he has passed a lonely childhood, brooding on fantasies. Like Hedvig, his grasp of reality is not firm, and so they become partners in a fatal *folie à deux*, the first of several in Ibsen. Intensities of unconscious subtextual exchange had been important in drama before this, but they had never *carried* the action; the plot of *The Wild Duck* simply will not work if we are not convinced that this buried encounter is taking place in the depths of Hedvig's imagination—if we don't feel it happening. And the encounter is fueled by histories and emotions from which Gregers, too, is alienated, including whatever vengeance he may be seeking on his father's bastard daughter (and perhaps even on his envied childhood hero, Hjalmar, who has become his father's protégé.)

The simultaneous projection of alienated subtexts, with all the risk and excitement it lends to performance, creates a whole new sense of encounter on the stage and summons a new kind of dramatic writing to make use of it. It should be stressed that this writing affects not only the psychological life of the actors but of the audience as well. We have already seen how in *The Master Builder* the varied and conflicting pulses of Solness's feelings about his powers combine with Herdal's and Hilda's provocations—and the audience's conflicted role as believers/disbelievers in the supernatural—to produce an uncanny shock. This in itself amounts to an exceedingly complex orchestration of half-guessed and competing psychological motifs, in which our own subtextual life may play a part. But even more powerful are the tremors set in motion throughout the play by the relation of Hilda and Solness. The whole of *The Master*

Builder depends on their subcutaneous sexual dialogue. Even their most symbolic flights—the "castles in the air," the "Viking spirit," the promised "kingdom" they speak of—are made concrete by the sexual currents between them. The meanings of these phrases shift, sometimes turning into their opposites even as they are spoken, depending on the subtext:

HILDA: (*full of life*): . . . We'll build the loveliest—the most beautiful thing anywhere in the world.

SOLNESS: (*caught up*): Hilda—tell me, what's that!

HILDA: (*looks smilingly at him, shakes her head a little, purses her lips, and speaks as if to a child*): Master builders, they are very—very stupid people.

SOLNESS: Of course they're stupid. But tell me what it is! What's the world's most beautiful thing that we're going to build together?

HILDA (*silent a moment, then says, with an enigmatic look in her eyes*): Castles in the air.

SOLNESS: Castles in the air?

HILDA (*nodding*): Yes, castles in the air! You know what a castle in the air is?

SOLNESS: It's the loveliest thing in the world, you say.

HILDA (*rising impatiently, with a scornful gesture of her hand*): Why yes, of course! Castles in the air—they're so easy to hide away in. And easy to build too. (*Look ing contemptuously at him*) Especially for builders who have a dizzy conscience. (848)

What Hilda means by "castles in the air" depends on Solness's response. Early in the dialogue the phrase suggests joyous fulfillment, later empty fantasy. They use symbols as real people under stress do, to conceal and reveal, attack and defend, often simultaneously.

The Master Builder is first of all a romance between an aging man and a very young woman, both of whom are psychologically volatile and suggestible, who feel a sexual spark between them that both frightens them and gives them desperately needed hope and purpose. At their first meeting, Solness tries to manipulate Hilda and becomes frightened, then excited, when she refuses to be dominated. When Hilda finds she can influence Solness she is thrilled, at one point depressed, then tremulously exalted. It is a relation in which fantasy ignites fantasy, where fear, recklessness, excitement, withdrawal goad one another on. That is where the life of the play lies—in the flow, more than half subterranean, of exchange.

It is in such dynamics that the realism of *The Master Builder* is to be found. If, as we have seen, projection is important in its psychology, it is important chiefly as a mechanism that operates in recognizable, familiar human exchanges. Thus while it may be accurate and useful to say, as Benjamin Bennett does, that Hilda is a "projection" of Solness,[4] she is so above all in the way people actually function as projections for each other in real life. It happens often enough, especially in intense sexual connections, and the key difference between this kind of relation and the simpler projections of fantasy (or of expressionism) is that in the relation between real individuals the projection is constantly unstable, subject to disruption, tension, countertransference. True, Hilda at moments speaks with the voice of Solness's mind, but it is Hilda, the specific individual, who is speaking. Her voice carries the dangerous inflections of her past, her needs, her desires.

II

In thinking about dramatic style in Ibsen, it is best to focus not on structural shapes or diction or the unfolding exposition but on what I would call the flow of *contacts* between performers. To my mind, the idea of contact vividly evokes the theatrical quality of Ibsen's mature prose drama.[5] But it is a kind of contact that takes place largely below the surface—not only below the bodily surface, below the skin and public face, but below the mental surface, below self-image and private expectation. Unconscious, half-conscious, subconscious, preconscious—all the terms we commonly use to try to evoke this large and varied realm—are inadequate, as they are in real life. In Ibsen's form of realism, contact with reality takes place in a buried topography of summits and abysses, thrills and terrors, which he came quickly to locate for performers in the new, alienated inwardness on which modern acting would be founded. Ibsen performance depends on achieving and sustaining this contact, conveying its tremors, incandescences, vertiginous plunges.

Understanding Ibsen depends on reading for the flow of contact. At the very least, this approach is a good way of overcoming the tendency to read Ibsen retrospectively, novelistically, condescendingly as one whose main theatrical skill is to provide a sleekly unfolding narrative. Indeed many passages in Ibsen that are easily overlooked or underread as merely connective turn out to contain exciting, exotic, unresolved struggles *about* contact. Thus the opening moments of *Ghosts* show us a (literally) dirty old man trying to get past a young housemaid's not-so-innocent defenses:

From the right side of the greenhouse, a door leads into the garden. Through the glass walls a somber fjord landscape can be glimpsed, half hidden by the steady rain.

ENGSTRAND is standing by the garden door. His left leg is partly deformed; under his bootsole he has a wooden block. REGINA, with an empty garden syringe in her hand, is trying to keep him from entering. (203)

The juxtaposition of garden room and grim landscape sets up a tension, an instability, that the whole play will elaborate—light and life are being invited in, but along with them, and looming larger, come darkness and cold. In this play that offers so many echoes of Greek tragedy, particularly *Oedipus Rex*, Ibsen has displaced Oedipus's deformed foot onto the carpenter, who seems to be forcing his way in to intimacy with his daughter. Regina's syringe is an oddly effective prop because of the unstable way it connects with other forces in the scene—water, glass, gardening, penetration, nature and nurture, inside and out. Waving it, Regina acts to protect the floor from her father's dripping clothes, the ears of the sleeping Osvald from her father's noise, her privacy from his questions:

REGINA (*in a low voice*): What do you want? Just stay
 where you are. Why, you're dripping wet.
ENGSTRAND: It's God's own rain, my girl.
REGINA: The devil's rain, it is!
ENGSTRAND: Jeez, how you talk, Regina. (*Hobbles a few
 steps into the room*) But now, what I wanted to say—
REGINA: Stop stomping about with that foot, will you!
 The young master's sleeping upstairs.
ENGSTRAND: Still sleeping? In broad daylight?
REGINA: That's none of your business. (203)

Regina is attempting to defend many vulnerable points at once: the tidy house of Alving, her independence from her father, a fragile, tentative class advantage over him, a possible future connection with Osvald that must be kept from Engstrand's view. Likewise Engstrand, in trying to get into the house, is exploring several possible advantages of his own, in addition to his little scheme for a sailors' brothel. What they are, he knows not, but he is ready to smell them out—and to "needle" Regina. All this is propelled by the hidden history of Regina's dead mother and her liaison with the late Captain Alving, which will be revealed in due course. But the point here is not the revelation. It is the comico-ugly instability of Regina's and Engstrand's variously hidden, partially alienated projects, the many motifs crowding toward the surface, the feints, the menace, the odd whiffs of greed, malice, and sexual cunning—an encounter all the more extraordinary in that it is a variation on the most hackneyed of theatrical openings: the servants' dialogue ("Nine o'clock and the master not down yet").

In this scene, resistance to contact and the threat of contact make for continual excitement and shifting of attack and advantage. It is an effective entry into a play where contact is increasingly felt as dangerous, infectious, incendiary—yet at the same time invited. Rain may be a threat, but, as the syringe indicates, the plants need water. Regina fights off her father, but there are moments of complicity as well as antagonism. And then, with Engstrand halfway through a proposal that carries a hidden sexual implication and a half-uttered threat, he suddenly turns insinuating, and we are unexpectedly contacted—by the dead. We hear the first ghost of the play:

ENGSTRAND: And when your mother got nasty, see—then I had to find something to needle her with. Always made herself so refined. (*Mimics*) "Let go of me, Engstrand! Leave me be! I've been three years in service to Chamberlain Alving at Rosenvold!" (205)

A dead woman is the first to speak the name of the dead man whose legacy will control the action, and her cry of Don't touch me! will echo through the play, as will its opposite (kiss me, let me embrace you, drink this champagne, join my brothel, put the pills in my mouth). This tense, grotesque, mysterious duel over contact has plunged us deep into the world of *Ghosts*.

A similar struggle opens the second act of *Hedda Gabler*. The heroine greets her old friend and confidant, the worldly, slightly sinister Judge Brack:

HEDDA, *dressed to receive callers, is alone in the room. She stands by the open glass door, loading a revolver . . .*

HEDDA (*looking down into the garden and calling*): Good to see you again, Judge!

BRACK (*heard from below, at a distance*): Likewise, Mrs. Tesman!

HEDDA (*raises the pistol and aims*): And now, Judge, I'm going to shoot you!

BRACK (*shouting from below*): No-no-no! Don't point that thing at me!

HEDDA: That's what comes of sneaking in the back way. (*She fires*).

BRACK (*nearer*): Are you out of your mind—!

HEDDA:Oh, dear—I didn't hit you, did I?

BRACK (*still outside*): Just stop this nonsense!

HEDDA: All right, you can come in, Judge. (722)

Again the setting reinforces a sense of ambiguous penetration from the outside and gives the defender a weapon. In more conventional terms, of course, the function of the scene is to "establish" both the pistol and Hedda's recklessness, and there will be more substantive duels with Brack later on. But the interplay, the way contact is negotiated, is ripely varied and suggestive. The effect can be largely humorous, heightened by the invisible Brack's sudden shift of tone and the contrast between our close-up view of Hedda and Brack's offstage exclamations. But any comedy will gain its life from the animus between them, the fear of being wounded (on both sides), the maneuvers over who makes the contact and who suffers it.

Brack enters, and there's opportunity to continue the comedy as he recovers himself. Once inside, however, he takes charge of the contact:

BRACK: Good God! Are you still playing such games? What are you shooting at?
HEDDA: Oh, I was just shooting into the sky.
BRACK (*gently taking the pistol out of her hand*): Permit me. (722)

The scene modulates into the deeper maneuvering of these perversely allied antagonists, marked by Ibsen's careful use of props to chart the effort to establish degrees of distance and intimacy:

HEDDA sits in the corner of the sofa. brack lays his coat over the back of the nearest chair and sits down, keeping his hat in his hand. A short pause. They look at each other.
HEDDA: Well?
BRACK (*in the same tone*): Well?
HEDDA: I spoke first.
BRACK (*leaning slightly forward*): Then let's have a nice little cozy chat, Mrs. Hedda.

HEDDA (*leaning further back on the sofa* ...) (723)

Later in the scene, when a visit from her former admirer Løvborg is anticipated, Hedda will move Brack's coat and hat, while Brack, discomfited, will make an effort to reclaim them. She is preparing access for Løvborg to the sofa, a crucial piece of furniture that she uses throughout this act to make, control, and limit contact, just as she has done in General Gabler's time.

These scenes echo melodramatic patterns that would have been familiar to Ibsen's audience; a more obvious version is Krogstad's visit to Nora in *A Doll's House*. Like him, both Brack and Engstrand resemble melodrama villains. But Ibsen's characters have a subtler life. They wound and are wounded in more complicated ways. In using them Ibsen is not writing melodrama but, in a sense, he is writing about melodrama, about the kind of emotional and cultural tension of which melodrama is an expression.

It is as though Ibsen grasped the fears and fantasies that made melodrama so appealing in his century—feelings that could only be discharged by a breathless encounter between extremes of good and evil. Behind melodrama is the kind of fear that haunts a Solness, a Hedda, an Allmers—but also, in more conventional form, the rigid Kroll, the prudish Manders, the reformed alcoholic Løvborg, even a Julian the Apostate. These characters inhabit a world—Or is it a body?—threatened, perhaps already infected, by some contagious weakness or subversion. It may be anything from a doctrine to an appetite—sexual desire, moral guilt, religious doubt, alcoholism. Like the two most notorious sources of *fin de siècle* anxiety, homosexuality and Jewishness, each may be felt as a taint that can destroy all who come in contact with it, an inner stain that may already be spreading through society.

Melodrama attempts to exorcise such fears by simplifying and externalizing the combat, making the contestants large and unambiguous. The villains of melodrama reflect in simplified form our hidden ambivalences and nightmares. Melodramatic typology is at home in Ibsen's realistic style because it speaks to the audience's own alienated subtexts. The plays engage the internal disturbances for which melodrama is a defensive projection. The power of a Krogstad lies in the fact that the superficial anxiety he arouses (Can little Nora escape his clutches?) taps into the profound anxieties about sex and marriage that threaten Ibsen's audience and which *A Doll's House* is implacably moving to confront. The anxiety underlying melodrama has a social as well as a psychological dimension: fear of a contact whose touch can shatter the sustaining structure, whether of a personality or a community. Deep contact in Ibsen performance is never very far from the sources of such anxiety.

III

There is another word that may help to describe the style and its implications. Ibsen uses it in a conversation with William Archer:

"It is much easier," he said, "to write a piece like *Brand* or *Peer Gynt*, in which you can bring in a little of everything, than to carry through a severely logical (*konsekvent*) scheme, like that of *John Gabriel Borkman*, for example."[6]

As Ibsen employs it, *konsekvent* can be translated in a number of unsurprising ways, but it can just as easily be made to carry a weight very suggestive for his art. As in English, *konsekvent* can suggest causal relationship, result, or serious result. As in German, it can also suggest logical consistency. Among other things, Ibsen here is clearly evoking the "rational" plotting, the linking of story elements characteristic of well-made dramaturgy, but remember that he is applying it to a very late play, which departs notably from well-made construction. The "logic" in *John Gabriel Borkman* has little to do with the intricate meshing of external events typical of *A Doll's House* and the other early plays in the realistic sequence; rather, its logic depends on character, psychology, intensity of focus. What is *konsekvent* about it is the achievement of an integrated, connected sequence, contact triggering contact, a concerting of pressures, a knitting together that is, in a non-Norwegian sense of the word which is nevertheless entirely appropriate to the effect Ibsen achieves, consequential, of an important magnitude (as in "a person of consequence"). This is a conception in which ethical and stylistic force are inseparable.

No Ibsen play can open in New York without some reviewer using the adjective "creaking" to describe its dramaturgy. This reflects a common prejudice against his plots, which we are now in a position to address. The standard description of Ibsen's style sees it as an application of old-fashioned Scribean plotting to an original and penetrating social and psychological analysis. Ibsen is, of course, understood to have put the mechanism to noble uses, purged it of coincidence, asides, and other excrescences, and gradually to have suppressed it in favor of deeper explorations of character. Nevertheless, it is implied, something of the old machinery always remains to taint the truth and realism of his creations. Even among his most sympathetic exponents, a trace of condescension is detectable, usually more than a trace. But the style is archaic only if we believe that Ibsen was trying to be Chekhov or Cesare Zavattini and, alas, never quite learned how. The idea of *konsekvent* style, with its use of constraint to produce ever more excruciating contact, suggests a different interpretation.

One sees this most readily by looking not at obviously inadequate readings of Ibsen but at some of the best. Francis Fergusson's comments on *Ghosts*, for instance, are justly famous. It is hard to think of a better example of criticism that is at once closely technical and powerfully philosophical—or of a better place to begin the study of Ibsen. No one has a finer appreciation of what Cocteau called the poetry of the theater—the way the large mechanisms of theatrical presentation can be handled with the subtlety and intensity of poetry. And no one has written better about what Fergusson calls the "hidden poetry" of

Ghosts. Yet even so, for Fergusson there is a kind of fault line in that play between Ibsen's theatrical craft and his most serious subject matter.

For Fergusson the suspenseful story and the thrilling series of emphatic climaxes that close each act are inadequate to *Ghosts*' poetic ambitions. They fail to articulate Mrs. Alving's spiritual quest or to invest her struggle to escape from the Alving past with the kind of philosophical, social, and emotional resonance we expect from great poems and classical tragedy.

Mrs. Alving is left screaming with the raw impact of the calamity. . . . The action of the play is neither completed nor placed in the wider context of meanings which the . . . purposes of poetry demand.[7]

Fergusson's is a refined version of the usual complaint that the plot of *Ghosts* is artificial, exaggerated, unreal, in short that it creaks. Behind this, as I have suggested, lies an assumption that the aim of Ibsen's dramaturgy is a convincingly literal realism, that the turns and climaxes of his plot amount to a sacrifice of this type of realism in favor of the shocks of bourgeois entertainment, especially what Chekhov (who thought *Ghosts* "a trashy play")[8] called the punch-in-the-nose ending.

Such comments ignore the historical fact that Scribean plotting is a product, and an equally original one, of the same era that introduces continuous surface realism to the theater—both emerging well before Ibsen. There is plainly a way, as yet never satisfactorily explained, in which, like the new interest in realistic description, Scribe's fascination with tightly meshed gears expressed some reality of modern life to the newly enlarged middle-class audience. Perhaps it was because this audience found itself grappling with a radically changed world in which vast, pervasive secular networks of cause and effect seemed to impinge on people's lives in everything from the stock market to railway schedules to the workings of that new secular force, "history." The technical ingenuities of the well-made play may have appealed to the audience by their benign mimicry of such processes. In any case, Ibsen's adaptation of Scribe was brilliant—above all it turned the edge of escapist entertainment against itself. Indeed self-delusion for an Ibsen character often takes the form of imagining one's life as a well-made play with a romantic moral. Both Nora and Helmer are victims of this kind of theatrical escapism, as are Hjalmar and Gregers in *The Wild Duck*. And Ibsen clearly wishes to foster the *impression* of tight, well-made logic, even when his plots no longer require it. In *The Master Builder*, the connection between Hilda's arrival and Ragnar's fate is not so strictly causal as that, say, between the arrival of Mrs. Linde, who gets Krogstad's old job, and Krogstad's now desperate ultimatum to Nora, but it is made to feel so. The dovetailing—Hilda with Ragnar's drawings, Hilda with Solness on the veranda, Ragnar appearing with a wreath, Ragnar and Hilda watching while Solness climbs—reinforces a sense of closely plotted logic in its efficient linking. Where Chekhov works to disguise the compactness of his narration, Ibsen seeks to underline it. The constraints of an apparently well-made plot resonate powerfully with the other elements of the *konsekvent* style.

Fergusson, in fact, is alert to the kind of integration that is characteristic of Ibsen's style, and especially to the way it operates most intensely at the performance level. For instance, in discussing *Ghosts* he focuses on the lengthy act 1 dialogue between Mrs. Alving and Pastor Manders and the many motifs it brings together. As a young bride, Helene had run away from her late husband, Captain Alving, to seek refuge with Manders, to whom she was attracted. Manders, scandalized, persuaded her to return. Now, stung by Manders's disapproval of her progressive ideas, she attacks the conservative values Manders associates with Alving and describes the full horror of the apparently happy later years of her marriage to a brutal, drunken debauchee. Mrs. Alving and Manders also clash over the upbringing of Osvald, who, when he appears, further shocks Manders by praising the bohemian lives of his fellow artists in Paris. Finally, as the act ends and Osvald is heard attempting to embrace the maid, Regina, in the next room, Mrs. Alving reveals to Manders that Regina is Alving's child.

Fergusson links the force of these unfolding complications to the way the scene is crafted for performance:

The main part of Act I . . . is a debate, or rather agon, between Mrs. Alving and the Pastor. . . . [Osvald's] appearance produces what the Greeks would have called a complex recognition scene, with an implied peripety for both Mrs. Alving and the Pastor, which will not be realized by them until the end of the act. But this tragic development is written to be acted; it is to be found, not so much in the actual words of the characters, as in their moral-emotional responses and changing relationships to one another.[9]

The intricate development of the action is carried subtextually by the acting. Indeed, there is no better example in Ibsen of how the resonances Fergusson associates with poetry—and finds lacking in *Ghosts*—emerge in *Ghosts* from the manipulation of its plot across the subtextual life of its actors. It is not necessary even to accept Fergusson's insistence on a rather narrowly defined "tragic rhythm" to see how the debate between Mrs. Alving and Manders over bohemianism and radical literature adds a richly complicating pressure to our sense of their dramatic relation.

Over the course of the act, amused and then angered by Manders, cheered and then troubled by her son, Mrs. Alving begins to understand more clearly her crusade to exorcise the Alving heritage, but it is an understanding clouded with increasing doubt. She is experiencing a rearrangement of her relation to her own experience. Half grasped, remembered and forgotten, it looms beneath the clearer alterations in her relation with Manders as they emerge in their debate. At the same time we undergo shifts in our own relation to the experience of the play. Not only is there a shifting emotional substrate to her argument with Manders but the clash of their positions is reinforced by a kind of metadramatic constraint on our understanding of the action. Our growing recognition of the dramatic function of their dialogue as a *debate*, that is, as a presentation of opposed intellectual positions, itself serves to increase dramatic tension. By advancing Mrs. Alving's status as representative of "new ideas," the play exerts yet another pressure on its own situation, forcing us to experience Mrs. Alving as the obscurely driven seeker of an as yet unknown illumination. Responding to a series of crises, she—and the other characters—will try urgently to formulate this illumination, for instance, as the idea of "ghosts" or the joy of life or even (suddenly and disconcertingly) as Captain Alving's own possible status as society's misunderstood victim[10]—but the idea which Mrs. Alving seeks to represent will always remain beyond formulation, an increasingly desperate pressing toward "the light," erupting in increasingly intense and contradictory embodiments as the fire in the orphanage that concludes act 2 and the deadly sunrise over the fjords as the play ends.

Ultimately the logic of the plot is neither realistic nor Scribean. That is, the concerting of its elements does not aim primarily either at sustaining an illusion of surface verisimilitude or providing the irresistible narrative drive, the *mouvement* which Scribe considered to be the aim and essence of all drama—though the play does well at both. Instead, Ibsen's treatment of incident is designed above all to intensify contact, to raise the stakes for Mrs. Alving, to transmit pressure to her and, through the anxieties of her performance, to put pressure on us.

Similarly the spectacular climaxes in *Ghosts* serve the ends neither of verisimilitude nor a punch in the nose but of psychological intensification. They anticipate a strategy we have already observed at the end of *The Master Builder*. Propelled, rhythmically, by the accumulating pressures of the dialogue, they project dammed-up internal forces on a tense and vivid external world. The effect is to join actors and audience in an uncanny burst of feeling. The scene in *The Master Builder* is in fact modeled on the climax of the second act of *Ghosts*, which Ibsen also reworks in *Little Eyolf*. In *Ghosts* the offstage fire in the orphanage breaks out at a moment of emotional crisis on stage, as Mrs. Alving prepares to reveal to Osvald and Regina that they are brother and sister. From a logical standpoint it interrupts the dialogue, but psychologically it completes it:

MRS. ALVING: Now I can speak out freely.

MANDERS: But you can't do that! No, no, no!

MRS. ALVING: I both can and will. And without demolishing any ideals.

OSVALD: Mother, what is it you're hiding from me?

REGINA: Mrs. Alving! Listen! People are shouting out there.

OSVALD: What's going on? What's that light in the sky?

REGINA (*cries out*): The orphanage—it's burning!

(258–59)

As with Solness's plunge to death in *The Master Builder*, the cries offstage and on and the violence they accompany seem to explode from the release of long suppressed psychological content. Mrs. Alving opens her mouth to speak the forbidden truth, voices are raised in anger and horror, and flames break forth, lighting up the sky. As realism it has been condemned as melodramatic, too convenient. But it is not realism in any narrow sense—it is a bold moment of expressionism way ahead of its time. And it works because it is *konsekvent.*

It seems hard for critics to see Ibsen's plotting as a *component* of style, a form of kinetic imagery designed to produce an effect in concert with a play's other elements. There is a tendency, starting well before Fergusson, to see the plot as an expedient, a way of delivering other, more important materials. From this point of view, the aim of plot is to get out of the way with as little distortion of reality as possible. Any pressure the plot imposes is likely to seem a limitation on Ibsen's artistry. Thus, as notably perceptive a critic as Richard Gilman registers the constraint accurately but seems to echo Fergusson in considering it a defect:

The machinery of plot works logically to establish necessary physical connections, more or less narrow sequences of cause and effect which propel the action forward but at the expense of a fullness of poetic significance. The poetry survives—it is what keeps the plays alive for our pleasure—but it is hemmed in, cramped; the trouble we have with these plays is that their plots keep crowding out their perceptions.[11]

But the narrowness Gilman describes is an indispensable part of the poetry. It contributes to the texture of anxiety. The "perceptions" of these plays, whether one assigns them to the characters or to the audience, have no meaning apart from all the things that "crowd" them. In fact the perceptions themselves are part of the crowding.

The famous letter in *A Doll's House* [Gilman continues], the father's pipe in *Ghosts*, Løvborg's manuscript in *Hedda Gabler*—quintessential objects of the well-made plot—have the effect of imposing on the plays a stringency, an inevitability of a smaller, more limited kind than Ibsen's imagination had conceived.[12]

Think, for a moment, of what it would be like for a designer to locate the second act of *A Doll's House* inside a huge letter box. Granted it would be weirdly, self-indulgently wrong—but the fault would not be one of misrepresentation. Rather it would be an overstatement of the obvious, the distracting exaggeration of a perfectly expressive image. The desperate tarantella Nora performs at the end of the act to distract her husband from discovering Krogstad's letter shows us, among other things, a songbird beating her wings against a cage of contingency. Løvborg may be right to consider his book a great contribution to knowledge, but his *manuscript* is an object that can plop grotesquely into a gutter and get passed through a series of incompetent hands until its even more grotesque reconstruction. In *Hedda Gabler* a terrifying whirl of unwieldy, mishandled objects (pianos, pistols, photograph albums) accompanies the characters' abrupt and often clumsy attempts to touch, manipulate, and evade one another. These objects are not McGuffins, interchangeable counters in a game whose aim is suspense and resolution. They powerfully and precisely concretize the world in which Ibsen's characters are forced to struggle. Indeed they often express the struggle itself.

Gilman is quite right to note the "stringency" of the process, but it is not the stringency of a neatly inevitable story, of a linking of clues, Agatha Christie-fashion. Rather it communicates an accelerating pressure, a succession of constraints that compel contact and encourage the intensities of a certain kind of acting. Pushed forward by this emerging system of constraints and contacts, the drama achieves its power to move and change us—not only through the increasing pressure of the situation but through what might be called formal or histrionic pressure on the actors, the escalating artistic demands for responsiveness their exchanges call for.

IV

The determinative force in Ibsen of this pressure of inwardness on inwardness has several important implications. The first, for performers, is that the life of buried interaction must be achieved at every instant. This is by now a "method" cliché, but it is usually honored in Chekhovian ways, and these by themselves are insufficient to make Ibsen come alive in the theater. All the Chekhovian specialties—the little riffs of oblique response, the velleities, hankerings, indirect traces of distant concerns, all the convincingly rumpled surfaces of daily life that contemporary actors, brought up on scenes from *Uncle Vanya* and *The Seagull*, are so good at conveying—may actually be present in an Ibsen production and still produce an unconvincing result. My own experience of Ibsen in performance is that there is usually a forced or rhetorical quality at key moments, or at least a missing of steps along the way. Without a continuous *sharp* pressure of buried interaction—it may properly be called "cruel" in the Artaudian sense—Ibsen production fails.

The failure is usually made manifest when a climactic event comes across as implausible, and then the critical verdict goes against the artificiality or melodrama of Ibsen's plots. But key moments like Hedvig's suicide depend on the unbroken series of alienated subtextual contacts that supports them. Michael Meyer has found an account of a performance of *The Lady from the Sea*, specifically the scene in which the heroine decides to remain with her husband, which seems to represent the solution of just this kind of problem in that play:

The objection [he writes] most commonly raised against *The Lady from the Sea* is the difficulty of making the climactical moment of Ellida's choice seem convincing. In this connection Dr Gunnar Ollén has written: "No one who saw the production in Vienna in the spring of 1950, with Attila Hörbiger as Wangel and Paula Wessely as Ellida, will share the opinion that Ellida's choice is implausible. The way Hörbiger played the scene in which he gives Ellida her freedom, her choice seemed utterly natural. He became red in the face, and had difficulty in enunciating his words, standing absolutely motionless and upright, with tears streaming down his cheeks. Quite simply, a stronger emotional power emanated from her husband than from the sailor. She . . . stared at Wangel as though seeing him for the first time, and then walked slowly across to him as though magnetically drawn. It was as if two hypnotists were fighting to gain control of a medium."[13]

What is plain here is the crucial role of intense, sustained subtextual dialogue. The critic has rendered the effect in a relatively crude way, but it is unmistakable. Admittedly it is always hard, and never very satisfying, to extract the sense of a live performance from a written description. Even quite full and particular accounts tend to capture the quality of individual portrayals rather than the moment-by-moment interplay between actors. (It is even hard to get a sense of this from videotapes of theatrical productions.) Thus I imagine that many widely admired performances, such as those described in Frederick and Lise-Lone Marker's extraordinary study, *Ibsen's Lively Art*,[14] may have surpassed Hörbiger and Wessely's *The Lady from the Sea* in effectiveness. But the description quoted has the rare virtue of being specific about subtextual interaction. And it seems to record a good instance of the contact needed to make one of the testing moments in Ibsen convincing.

Emotional power by itself is not enough. Shaw, for

instance, correctly points out that the lovers in *Rosmer-sholm* must "sustain the deep black flood of feeling from the first moment to the last"[15]—but, as we shall see in a later chapter, the true flood in *Rosmersholm* is not something that comes pouring out of one actor or the other. It is the product, as it were, of many colliding tides, the cross currents and sudden crestings, the rips and whirlpools of combined and conflicting torrents. This is why—though many Ibsen actors certainly overwhelm their audiences, at least at moments, with the flood of their emotions—they seldom sustain them from first to last or do so in unpersuasive ways. Even if the emotion is authentic, its connection to the action is not, and it leaves the audience blaming Ibsen's artificiality.

There is a second implication here for readers and critics. The flow of contacts is the stuff of the play; it is the major sensuous component of the play's effect in the theater, and, as such, it must be a primary object of interpretation. Just as one does not simply read a dog or a tree or an artist's smock in a Rembrandt painting but reads the way he paints them, so we must read the brushwork of performance life enabled and required by Ibsen's text. In scenes like those between Gregers and Hedvig, Rosmer and Rebecca, Hilda and Solness, Rubek and Irene, we must feel buried desires and forgotten traumas fitting each other, finding each other out, igniting each other, forcing the characters to desperate acts. These are scenes that, to be convincing, must not be expository but frighteningly interactive.

I would hope, finally, that one further point has been suggested by this discussion—that it is very dangerous to assimilate Ibsen to any general model of dramatic naturalism. It is true, of course, that some of my remarks about subtext and anxiety apply equally well to other dramatists, indeed to much modern drama beyond the precincts of naturalism. But the kind of style and subtextual activity I have been describing is, as we have seen, quite different from that of Chekhov or Arthur Miller or Tennessee Williams, particularly in its emphasis on constriction, on a certain kind of pressure relentlessly applied. It is not to be viewed as part of a general project to achieve a more transparent or less "artificial" rendering of ordinary behavior. From such a perspective, I fear, Ibsen is all too often seen as a kind of model-T Chekhov. But the tight plotting, the spectacular climaxes, the emotional velocity, the well-made devices are totally misunderstood if viewed as excrescences or throwbacks—flaws in some primitive science of realism soon to be superseded by a thousand plays and films. They take their place, along with the more apparently literal or photographic elements of Ibsen's drama, in a carefully judged formal ensemble. They are parts of a unique dramatic style, as demanding in its restrictions and integrated in its effects as Sophocles' or Racine's.

CHAPTER THREE

Style as Vision: The Wild Duck, *Child Abuse, and History*

THE CHARACTERISTIC BRACING intensity of Ibsen's dramatic vision—the sense of torpedoing the ark—owes much to the stylistic rigor described in the last chapter. But how, specifically, do style and vision connect? How does the texture of constraint, of constriction and anxiety, the insistence on a constant pressure of subtextual contacts, translate into a sentiment of being, a feeling about life and society? How do the local dramatic effects in Ibsen become a comprehensive effect, a sustained impact that takes on the force of meaning—and how can this meaning be described in terms that are true to the effect? There are, of course, many possible answers, but in the next two chapters I explore what I take to be an exemplary one, a subject that perhaps more than any other brings us close to the heart of Ibsen's method, to the place where his sense of drama and of the human condition join—the subject of child abuse.

Ibsen's treatment of characters who are hurt, molested, or exploited in childhood offers not only a clue to a central vibration—arguably *the* central vibration—in Ibsen's vision of society but constitutes a particularly revealing instance of how the dramatic texture of his work transforms and inflects his subject matter. Indeed, if in looking at abused children in Ibsen we are comfortable with using a word like *vision* to describe his presentation of human affairs, it is because vision itself is a motif Ibsen explicitly associates with this subject—vision both in its most literal sense and as an inescapable metaphor for a certain kind of theatrical effect.

I

The wounded child peers at us through all the luxuriant growth of nineteenth-century literature, from Blake to Dostoevsky, from Dickens to Rimbaud. And the wound is a mark of power and horror, a ministry of fear felt as transformingly in Freud as in Wordsworth. Ibsen grasps the centrality of the subject as well as anyone in the century. There are a lot of damaged children in his work, and it is not hard in every case to see a sexual dimension in the damage.[1] There are Hilda Wangel and Eyolf Allmers and Hedvig Ekdal and Osvald Alving. There are also Hedda, General Gabler's daughter, the pliable young Johannes Rosmer, so influenced by his tutor and his violent father, and possibly Rebecca West (Who knows how young she was when Dr. West made his first advances?). There is Nora Helmer, passed on from father to husband. We will see that Ibsen's treatment of such injuries is perhaps the most comprehensive of all. But first it is important to locate the theme historically.

Did Europe in the nineteenth century begin to abuse its children as never before, or did it rather begin to acknowledge how widespread that abuse was, indeed that its culture might be founded on child abuse? The question is, of course, unanswerable, but unanswerable in a way that goes to the heart of child abuse because it reproduces the cruel undecidability inherent in the crime.[2] The history of child abuse can never be written because the abuse itself is inscribed in fantasy, in the intertwined fantasies of victim, abuser, and observer, because the reader of any such history is trapped inside the fantasy in which the abuse has its defining life.

This is not to deny the physical reality of assaults on children—but the physical reality of abuse is rarely the point. *As* a physical reality abuse is simply that, assault. The radical damage of child molestation goes far beyond the physical damage, which may indeed be nonexistent. It takes place in the determining mental life of the child, in the imagination, or rather at the base of the imagination—and it is on such foundational traumas to the imagination that the mental life of the adult is built. This is as true of the less specifically sexual examples of child abuse—child labor, the deprivations and oppressions of family life—as it is of molestation itself.

The nineteenth century seems to become aware of all these abuses—either seeing abuse everywhere as a social problem, a new evil born of industrialism, or perhaps simply discovering it in its heart. The question is unanswerable: Did Halvard Solness pause on his upwardly mobile track to commercial success to crush an impressionable thirteen-year-old girl to his body and kiss her on her lips, or was there simply a moment when, simultaneously, she imagined it and he desired it? We never know, we *can* never know, but it destroys them both.

It is useful here to recall another damaged child whose appearance in a long-unpublished play by a precocious German medical student uncannily anticipates not only Ibsen but the whole course of modern drama. At the end of Büchner's *Woyzeck*, Woyzeck's bastard child is playing horsie. He does not yet know or perhaps does not understand that his father—tormented, exploited, cruelly experimented on by his superiors—has murdered his mother. The other children jeer at him:

CHILDREN: Hey you, your mother is dead! . . .
CHILD: Hop! Hop!
CURTAIN

The child's mother is dead, his father sure to be executed. Whatever future we can contemplate at this moment hangs on this child. Do we feel hopeful, sympathetic, repelled, crushed, numb? Where is the story going, where does it leave us? In a word, what is the force of this ending?

Probably the first matter to consider is that we do not know if this *is* the ending of *Woyzeck*. Büchner left his manuscript unfinished at his death, and the order of the scenes cannot be determined with certainty.[3] But this undecidability seems part of its force. It works most powerfully of all the possible endings because, as Berg saw, when he placed the scene at the end of his operatic version, it so well soaks up the uncertainty. There is a doubt or question *inside* the rightness of its focus.

The child offers an undefended surface to an obscure and threatening process that seems recognizably modern. His figure, at risk, innocent, but almost sinister within its innocence, seems so easily to absorb the entire chronicle of complex abuse which Büchner has made out of the story. It juxtaposes the child with all the social and psychological forces that have pushed Woyzeck toward his crime, and with the unspecified consequences of the crime still to come. One modern name for the process the child confronts is history.

Büchner's first play, *Danton's Death*, written a year earlier when he was twenty-one, was about the French Revolution. *Woyzeck* is set a generation later, in the Germany of Büchner's own day, and the child seems easily a figure for history's victim. But he seems also a bad seed from which history may explode. The implied sense of history here is new. For it is not a sense of history as fate or as conflict or even as a chain of events that is evoked by this child, but rather of history as an obscure weave of forces. What lies behind it is the distinctly modern notion of history as a certain kind of scientific construct, a complex causal process whose secular explanation it is the burden of modern consciousness to undertake. This notion of history seems to emerge in Western thought as a response to the French Revolution.

The French Revolution offered a new model for anxious

political reflection—of an inexplicable secular cataclysm of which we were all descendants. More precisely, it was the model of an unexplained catastrophe that nevertheless should be explicable. It was a secular event and evidently the result of a play of forces of exactly the type that enlightened secular thought considered susceptible to analysis.

For Marx, the French Revolution was the event that necessitated the life project of historical explanation. No previous moment in history had created a burden of comparable difficulty, and it is no surprise that vast systems, like Hegel's, of making sense of events as parts of a historical process emerge so soon after the revolution and are so full of the shockwaves it unleashed.

A distinctive feature of the French Revolution was that the event seemed to move as if to an agenda of its own. Not God's agenda; by then there could be no patience with such an explanation. Yet it did not seem governed by man's agenda either, though clearly a horde of intentions had flooded into it. Nevertheless it was not just a disturbance, a stone thrown into the pool of time. Rather it had momentum, direction, logic, as if propelled by something embedded in the very process of its unfolding, a life of its own. A life to be attributed to history itself, to be explained by a science of what shaped history.

Let us think again of *Woyzeck* ending with Woyzeck's bastard child riding/being carried on his imaginary horse, fading away, a final silhouette of the drama. Is he the product, the pathos, or the source of the process we have been witnessing? How can we tell the dancer from the dance? At this moment we may remember that the Yeats poem "Among School Children," from which this famous evocation of undecidability is taken, is also about children and what happens to them in the adult world:

O chestnut tree, great rooted blossomer,
Are you the leaf, the blossom, or the bole?
O body swayed to music, o brightening glance,
How can we know the dancer from the dance?[4]

Yeats's question and his poem refer, of course, to history and society and the unappeasable restlessness of human desire, but they are also the end of a sequence of "questionings" in which figures of adult power and sexual intensity have hovered over children, concerned to draw meaning, energy, radical satisfaction from them.

In Yeats, as in Büchner, troubled by the image of a vulnerable child, we find ourselves confronting history. We could take a similar path through Wordsworth's long autobiographical poem, *The Prelude*, where the young man, shocked by the cruelties of the revolution, overstimulated by the experience of urban crowds, reconstitutes himself as a poet by remembering moments of overwhelming childhood stimulation by "nature"—a nature figured as threatening, beautiful, parental, as ravished and ravishing, sometimes menacingly external, sometimes thrillingly internal to the poet/child. Or we could connect Dostoevsky's memory/fantasy of the raped child in the bathhouse to his tormented relation with Western "Enlightenment." The point is that, regularly, wound round the figure of the wounded child we find an anxiety about history, society, and the self that rises from the traumas of the French Revolution and anticipates some of the central questions of modern culture. The child functions as a center of fantasy in which we are all implicated, all betrayed.

We can, then, usefully distinguish two aspects of child abuse in nineteenth-century thought (and indeed in the thought of our own century) that will figure in our exploration of Ibsen. First, the figure of the wounded child as the intersection of many strands of social investigation. Second, this child as a peculiarly empowering figure, whose wound speaks for us and to us not simply of guilt and/or desire but of a power to engage, even to change the secret life of our times.

II

Child abuse is an almost obsessive theme in Ibsen, and its resonance in his drama is revealingly illuminated by a curious feature of the way he represents it. I am referring to the fact that in the two plays in which Ibsen brings a damaged child onstage and extensively presents the child's sufferings, he links the subject to an equally extensive imagery of sight and seeing.

To be a poet is to *see*, said Ibsen famously. It is a claim that has powerful relevance for his theatrical art. The world his "realistic" plays show us is insisted upon in massive, seamless visual detail. We are made responsible for seeing every square inch of the stage. Instead of paying attention to a few selected props (a crown, a skull) as we are on Shakespeare's stage, we must be aware of every object in continuous, real-space relation to every other object. The latest books are on the round table in the center of a parlor that looks out into another room, full of plants, beyond which we see a fjord.

At the same time, seeing, for Ibsen, implies a powerful ethical force, as even the preceding account of visual realism suggests. We have already had occasion to refer to Ibsen's other famous epigram about poetry:

Å *dikte,*—det er å holde
dommedag over seg selv.

To write poetry—or plays—is to hold a doomsday judgment on oneself. If to be a poet is to see, then for Ibsen it is a kind of seeing that implies a pitiless intensity of self-examination.

But one can go much further than this and approach Ibsen by trying, quite specifically and concretely, to understand the *dramatic* dimension of his pitiless gaze, what it means as a material aspect of his technique, a crucial part of the large, comprehensive effect we recognize in his drama. And here we will be helped most by looking at the interplay in his work between the motifs of seeing and of childhood suffering. For much of the harsh power of Ibsen flows from a complex sense of seeing attached to the figure of the wounded child and reinforced by the exigencies of his dramatic style. In his plays it is as if we saw and were seen with a vision that draws its energy from the wounds themselves—we stare, we are stared at, we see with the victim's eyes, we see the abuse, we see ourselves as abusers, we see our abusers, all with a vengeful, liberating, unblinking ruthlessness.

III

Produced in 1884, five years after *A Doll's House* had catapulted Ibsen into European recognition, *The Wild Duck* left many in its audience confused. Perhaps no play in the past two centuries had so disconcertingly mixed comedy with painful emotional content. Equally disconcerting was the way it directed much of its mockery at a figure who seemed to embody Ibsen's own presumed zeal for social reform. Gregers Werle, the rebellious son of a rich businessman, attaches himself to the family of his old friend, Hjalmar Ekdal, urging them to follow a program of honesty and truth in all things, especially their own relationships. Gregers's bungling efforts to persuade the vain and self-dramatizing Hjalmar to follow his "summons to the ideal" would seem comical except that they lead to the suicide of Hjalmar's beloved, if carelessly exploited daughter, Hedvig. Bewildered by Gregers's insistence that she sacrifice her pet wild duck to prove her love for her father, the fourteen year old turns the pistol on herself.

The Wild Duck abounds with references to sight and seeing. We are frequently reminded that the Ekdal family's living room, where most of the action takes place, doubles as a photographic studio. The reference to photography has seemed to many to suggest the superior accuracy of realism, and Ibsen did at one point refer to himself as a photographer but the emphasis is much less on the reality of what is seen than on distortions of the visual process. Hedvig Ekdal may have inherited her weak eyes from Gregers's father, for old Werle was her mother's lover, but it is Hjalmar who endangers her sight by allowing her to take over his work retouching photographs. As in his earlier plays, Ibsen makes the movement of the plot feel initially like a movement to enlightenment, but, even more deeply than in *Ghosts*, the enlightenment, when it appears, proves ambiguous. The ending of *Ghosts* might be considered a version of "tragic" illumination; like Oedipus, Helene Alving presses insistently toward a truth that proves shattering. In *Ghosts* we may wonder whether the discovery is worth the effort, but—at least at first glance—we do not doubt that it is a discovery. In *The Wild Duck* it is not clear whether anything has been discovered at all. A child is destroyed, and the competing "insights" offered at the play's end are no less fictive and distorted than the confused symbolic identifications that have driven her to suicide.

The method of the play becomes clear if we try to express its action in terms of a spine. It will be recalled that a spine, as we have defined it, is a single infinitive phrase, the more concrete the better, which describes with equal accuracy the dominant motivation or "through-line" of each of a play's major characters. To my mind, the most concrete infinitive phrase that can be accurately applied to all the characters in *The Wild Duck* is *to make the picture come out right*—to adjust reality so that it "looks good," as when one retouches a photograph.

Though its hero is a photographer, we never actually see anyone take a picture in *The Wild Duck*. Instead we witness a few brief, cranky discussions of the business side of photography, one momentary evocation of the social ambiguity of the photographer's position (Is Hjalmar being patronized at Werle's dinner?) and a single encounter with a photographic subject—significantly, the customers are invisible and are being assured by his wife, Gina, that they will receive their pictures soon, which stresses the gap between taking and making the picture. Above all, however, we see the work that seems to fill the gap, the work of retouching. So photography in the play is largely a matter of making the picture come out right, the way the customer wants or the photographer deems beautiful. That is the effort, the recurrent action, that the play's characters have in common, often with a quite literal visual component.

Hjalmar's occupation as a retoucher clearly extends to all the narratives by which he constructs and justifies his life. In the second act we see him telling the story of the dinner we have witnessed, so that what seemed painfully embarrassing in the first act now appears in a favorable light. His daughter and wife cooperate in this; indeed they work always to soothe him, to make him look good, to allow him a vision of himself as breadwinner, scientific genius, self-sacrificing father. Both Hjalmar and his father are given to grandiloquent, literary phrases that lend their lives an aura of romance and heroism. Gregers accuses his own father of trying to compose a false picture ("Tableau of father with son" [409]) but is equally guilty of trying to make a picture come out right in his portrait of Hjalmar as a man of unusual moral qualities. The sardonic Dr. Relling, with his theory of the "life-lie," claims to see a similar process of self-delusion at work universally, but even this theory allows Relling to retouch some unflattering features of his own existence.

There is an unusual amount of repairing, rearranging, and tidying up in the play. It begins, for example, with servants straightening up Werle's den for the party. We see Gina and Hedvig cleaning up their living quarters on several occasions (including at the end of act 2, where the sleeping Ekdal is carried off to bed), and the offstage mess she has to set to rights in Gregers's room is vividly described. To this may be added Hjalmar's careful piecing together of the document he has torn apart.

One important version of making the picture come out right is the composition of little playlets designed to reinforce some illusion a character wants to cherish. Gregers persuades Hedvig to kill the wild duck in order to convince her father that she loves him, and after the offstage shot rings out in act 5, Gregers and Gina join forces to convince Hjalmar of this scenario. But perhaps the most elaborate and pointed example of the process occurs immediately afterward, when Hedvig is brought in dead.

Here Ibsen gave careful thought to the composition of his own stage picture, as his direction suggests:

HJALMAR, GINA, and GREGERS drag HEDVIG into the studio; her right hand hangs down and her fingers curve tightly around the pistol. (487)[5]

This arresting visual focus serves mainly to sharpen our awareness of the various interpretive operations directed *at* it, each to some degree self-serving, each an attempt to make the picture we are observing make the "right" kind of sense.

Hjalmar's first effort, not surprisingly, stresses his own importance: the child died out of love for him. But this presents him in too cruel a light, so he quickly shifts the emphasis to himself as the victim of a cruel god:

And I drove her from me like an animal! And she crept terrified into the loft and died out of love for me! (*Sobbing*) Never to make it right again! Never to let her know—! (*Clenching his fists and crying to heaven*) Oh, you up there—if you *do* exist. Why have you done this to me?

Gina offers a simple religious explanation in terms of guilt:

We just didn't deserve to keep her, I guess.

Molvik, who is drunk, turns to a theological cliché:

The child isn't dead; she sleepeth.

They next turn from figurative to literal vision, from the moral to the visual aspects of the picture. Hjalmar offers a poetic impression:

There she lies, so stiff and still.

Relling tries physically to change the effect:

(*Trying to remove the pistol*) She holds it so tight, so tight.

Gina reasonably objects to this piece of retouching:

No, no, Relling, don't break her fingers. Let the gun be.

We may remember how Hjalmar has irritably tried to touch up Gina's speech by getting her to call it a "pistol." Now Hjalmar and Gina bend their attentions to displaying the body in what they consider an appropriate manner:

HJALMAR: She should have it with her.
GINA: Yes, let her. But the child shouldn't lie displayed out here. She ought to go into her own little room, she should. Give me a hand, Hjalmar. (488–89)

And they carry her off to another setting, as they carried off old Ekdal at the end of act 2, leaving Molvik, Relling, and Gregers to continue the battle over how to view her death. (From the point of view of accuracy and self-deception in seeing, it is interesting that during the scene with Hedvig's body, two of the characters on stage are drunk and two others are suffering from a hangover. Everyone in this scene is having difficulty trying to see straight.)

Broken up into its components like this, the threnos over Hedvig's body seems to highlight the savagely comic aspect of Ibsen's art, but the lament is poignant, too, and the pain, the tragic weight, derives from what underlies Ibsen's interest in *seeing* in this play.

In *The Wild Duck*, seeing is not so much a question of what is to be seen but of what is behind the eyes, of whose eyes one sees with:

You've seen me with your mother's eyes.... But you should remember that those eyes were—clouded at times. (409)

As this speech of old Werle's suggests, "making the picture come out right" is not only a matter of hypocrisy or convenient self-deception. It rises from the cloudiest springs of human disposition, from our most crippling needs and passions. "Seeing" as a determinative activity, as a crucial component of agency, is subtextual—buried and alienated in its origins, doing its fatal work in secret. Just as the play, for all its humor, is not simply comic, so the drive to retouch is located by Ibsen not simply in the human comedy of saving appearances or in the relatively conscious motors of self-interest but in deep and deeply deformed sources of imagination and desire. A child is at the center of *The Wild Duck* because the adult efforts at retouching that shape its action are all linked to the volatile and distorted psychic life we bring with us from childhood.

We come to understand this in part through the childhood histories of certain characters—Hedvig, Gregers, Hjalmar—and we feel it through the powerful subtextual currents Ibsen requires of his actors, but we also experience it in our own visual efforts with the stage picture— notably with its most spectacular feature. For there is a major element in the stage set that is constantly changing its appearance, constantly distracting and teasing us with altering contours and valences. Huge, complex, partially obscured, located at the back of the stage where it cannot help being noticed but cannot fully be observed, the garret where the duck is housed in an artificial forest literally upstages the photographer's studio. It is at once ludicrous and romantically evocative.

What is usually forgotten in discussions of the stage set in *The Wild Duck* is the way it engages the audience, the way it arouses our own not always fully conscious activity as spectators. In this case, it is an activity particularly concerned with the effort to see. We do not simply *respond* to the loft room (as we do, say, to the fjord scene glimpsed at the back of the *Ghosts* set); we try to look at it. There are things there we cannot quite see but wish to see, even when we are supposed to be looking somewhere else. It is the most complex and subtle stage set ever devised, certainly without parallel in theatrical history at the time Ibsen created it. He suggests its complexity—its dynamic engagement with the audience—in the stage directions:

The doorway opens on an extensive, irregular loft room with many nooks and corners, and two separate chimney shafts ascending through it. Clear moonlight streams through skylights into certain parts of the large room; others lie in deep shadow. (425)

Morning sunlight shines through the skylights. A few doves fly back and forth; others perch, cooing, on the rafters. Chickens cackle now and then from back in the loft. (433)

Not only does the loft look different at different times of day—a feature it shares with the set as a whole, and on which Ibsen insisted in his discussions with the original producers[6]—but it keeps us looking and noticing. We see it in at least four different lights. It invites curiosity, theatrical wonder, mixed feelings. The irregularity, the nooks and corners, the moonlight and shadow evoke romantic associations but also an effort to peer into what is not clearly seen—in part because it is not clearly lit, in part because it is at the back, beyond our clearest view, in part because of the way the characters describe it. The birds and animals moving around in it (or even simply asleep, as we are told they are when we first see the loft) are both an attraction and distraction. We will look for them, strain to see them, glance away to follow their flight or movement even when something is going on in the foreground, some necessary question of the play on which we should be focusing. We forget what we should remember and remember what we wish to forget. It is a process something like thinking over one's personal history or trying to recover a dream—the uncertain, groping attempt to separate fantasy from memory.

The play of light and dark and of animal life off in the background, as we strain to see it, makes it mysterious, fascinating, "a world of its own" as Hedvig calls it. Yet at the same time the loft is associated with a sense of delusion, self-deception, failure, pathetic limitation. We are watching not bears in a forest but rabbits in an urban attic, a piece of ingenious yet amateur carpentry, filled with the cackling of chickens as well as the cooing of doves, a source of embarrassment as well as interest for Hjalmar and Gregers, something which, like all live animals in the theater, both heightens and threatens the illusion, an effect that reminds us simultaneously of theater-as-magic and theater-as-contraption.

Hedvig finds it a mysterious and wonderful world, and thus it is associated with the rich, volatile imagination of a sensitive adolescent on the threshold of sexual maturity. But it is also something her father has made, and though, as such, it is an escape from his responsibilities (we see him tinkering with it when he should be retouching photographs), at the same time it shows Hjalmar at his best, the little boy who loves constructing toylike mechanisms. And our involuntary engagement as spectators in this huge contraption implicates us in his escapism. Indeed why should we call it involuntary, since we have come to the theater, the place of such "realism" and ingenuity, of our own free will?

The attic, then, combines the shabbiness and deceit of theater with its transfiguring power. It operates as a kind of reminder of the mental life we bring with us from childhood—the imaginative background which, poisoned and enfeebled as it may be, continues to affect us through our adult life. One process that seems everywhere figured in *The Wild Duck*, that seems central to Ibsen's view of life and that perhaps becomes clear to him for the first time as he writes this play, is that of people coming up injured from the depths of childhood.

The primary examples of this process are, of course,

Hedvig, Gregers, and Hjalmar, and part of the play's originality lies in the way it shows the two adults drawing on their own childhood injuries to damage the child fatally. To show us this—to make this kind of process visible for the first time onstage—Ibsen made new demands on his actors. We have already seen the kind of subtextual contact on which the pivotal scenes between Gregers and Hedvig depend.

We must not forget that, like Hedvig, Gregers is also an abused child. As Ibsen says in his work notes for the play, Gregers "experiences the child's first and deepest sorrows— sorrows of family—everyday anguish of family life." Hedvig was the name of Ibsen's sister, the one member of his family to whom he felt close. And he has given to Hedvig many details from his own childhood experience, especially of the fantasy world into which he withdrew. In *The Wild Duck* she pores over the very books that fascinated Ibsen as a child. But in the play Ibsen has made her brother—made himself, that is—into a stepbrother, a twisted and vengeful character, responsible for a suicide which, like little Eyolf's a decade later, punishes a self-absorbed, sensual parent.

In the end Hedvig is particularly vulnerable because she has been brutally and inexplicably rebuffed by her father. To win back his love, she is ready to accept Gregers's suggestion that she kill the duck; the sacrifice of something so precious to her will convince Hjalmar that she loves him. Just before she fires the shot, she overhears Hjalmar say, "If I asked her then: Hedvig, are you willing to give up life for me? (*Laughs derisively*) Yes, thanks—you'd hear all right what answer I'd get!" (486). At that moment she kills herself. So Hedvig's death is the result of her father's selfish mixture of affection and indifference, of the intimacy Gregers establishes and then manipulates, of the sexual secrets and suspicions that circulate through her household.

But there is also a social dimension to her victimization. Exploited like many child laborers, she endangers her eyes (and thus becomes more isolated) so that Hjalmar may live in relative leisure. His sudden anger at her is heightened by his suspicion that he in turn has been exploited by the wealthy Werle. Indeed the fantasy world of the garret is a compensation for the Ekdals' descent in class, which has closed the forests to them and locked them in a shabby urban life. Gregers, moreover, sees himself as a social reformer (he began his career distributing pamphlets to his father's employees), but his projects become increasingly identified with the bitterness he has carried with him since childhood and with his fatal, unseeing assault on Hedvig's imagination.

With Gregers, as with all the characters, one gets the sense of two juxtaposed modes of action: the relatively conscious effort to adjust the picture—to reform, meddle, tidy up, arrange, and interpret life; and a more unconscious, as it were subtextual, stumbling or groping in the depths. There is a strong premonitory image of the second kind of action early in the play, at the end of act 1:

GREGERS: Look—your gentleman friends are playing blindman's buff with Mrs. Sørby. . . . (*Laughter and joking from the company, which moves into view in the inner room*). (409–10)

The image is not only memorable; over the course of the play it operates in a kind of time-delayed subterranean manner, its meanings shifting and looming, quite literally in the background. Physically it occupies the stage space that will become the garret room in the succeeding acts. The space has remained brightly lit and largely unoccupied for most of act 1, which now closes on the arresting picture of a dozen well-dressed, well-fed adults groping about blindly in a child's game in this large light-filled area. The audience, at this point, may tentatively assign the image a rather superficial satirical, socially "progressive" meaning, easy mockery of the local plutocrats. This might well be the way Gregers would see it, and we tend to see things with his eyes at this moment in the play. But the image carries more power than that. The light-filled room initiates a suggestion that will be heightened by both the duck and the garret and by what we come to share of the characters' lives. It will remain in the audience's memory, half-forgotten, perhaps disconcertingly remembered, and as we struggle with what are now its half-lit nooks and crannies, the memory of that brightly lit pantomime of blindness is likely to seem more poignant and prophetic. For if it is true that we all come up injured from the depths of childhood, we also retain something of childhood's magic—something of its wildness, expansiveness, mystery, authenticity, though in wounded or tainted form. Life for all of us is a blindman's buff, a child's game now played by clumsy grown-ups whose groping mocks and mimes the lonely bewilderments of childhood. And that is both the comedy and the pity of it.

Coming up from childhood we enter history—and *The Wild Duck*, with its class conflicts, reform pamphlets, new inventions, and Darwinian imagery, is full of references to historical process and the forces that drive it. In Gregers and Hedvig, ambiguously linked figures of reformer and victim, we see a tormented image of social action which will be increasingly explored in the plays that follow. The hero of *Rosmersholm*, Ibsen's next play, will be a more plausible though equally flawed reformer, with an equally damaging childhood legacy. *Hedda Gabler* will bring on-stage, in Eilert Løvborg, a recognizably modern analyst of history with all the grand theoretical ambitions of a Hegel or Marx, and then follow the material fate of his theory as embodied in his manuscript, which is lost, then destroyed, then ineptly reconstructed, a grimly unpromising example of historical process. Solness's homes for human beings and Borkman's grandiose capitalist schemes will also be subject to devastating analysis. Above all, there will be *Little Eyolf*, to which we now turn. This is arguably Ibsen's cruelest play; certainly it is his most painful and sexually skewed representation of childhood. It also contains his most unforgettable images of sight, and it ends with yet another dubious plan for social reform, this time a project aimed directly at children. Their cries of pain, anger, and horror rise to our ears more than once in the play, from the margins of a cruelly indifferent sea.

CHAPTER FOUR

Eyolf's Eyes: Vision and Vengeance in Little Eyolf

"TO BE A POET IS ABOVE ALL TO SEE." But what, in this world of blindman's buff, does it mean, to see? What promise, ethical or aesthetic, does it offer? If every adult is a wounded or tainted child, who tends to see things with the wounded and tainted eyes of those who initially abused him, what kind of revealing or redeeming vision is possible? And who in the end is doing the seeing that constitutes the play? All dramatic performance theatricalizes its audience; any play casts *us*, usually in an amalgam of roles, some drawn from the cast of characters, others from the idea of an audience that the play projects. An audience watching *Murder in the Cathedral*, say, is playing a very different part from the same audience watching *What the Butler Saw*. So when we watch an Ibsen play, who are we when we "see," who sees for us, as us? Such questions will help to determine exactly how significant the idea of *seeing* is to Ibsen's dramaturgy, especially as it works itself out in one of his most difficult plays.

I

In the last two acts of *Little Eyolf* (1894), Alfred and Rita Allmers are tormented by an image of their dead son, the crippled Eyolf, who wandered away from them and drowned while they were absorbed in their own problems. The event is all the more painful because it echoes an earlier moment of neglect. Ten years before the play begins, Alfred and Rita, absorbed in lovemaking, left the infant Eyolf alone, sleeping on a table from which he fell and crippled himself. It is the mark of this wound, the boy's crutch, that floats to the surface of the fjord at the end of act 1 to signal Eyolf's drowning, accompanied by the grotesque shout—also a vivid visual image—of "Krykken flyter" (the crutch is floating) from the ragged children on the shore. What haunts both parents, however, what they cannot help seeing, is a vision of Eyolf's eyes. "The eyes, the eyes," cries Allmers, and it is this fierce impression of Eyolf's accusatory gaze that breaks him, as it breaks his wife.

It is not hard to read *Little Eyolf* as a child's fantasy of vengeance on his parents through suicide, a notion that becomes irresistible if we know anything of Ibsen's life and other work. Feeling neglected, shut out from the parental circuit of love, the child imagines, "How they would suffer if I died; then they would regret how they have treated me, then I would be even with them for what they have done."

Fueled by *Little Eyolf*, we may think of Ibsen's theater as the seeing place for a child's vengeance, where the force of the action is a kind of seeing vengeance *on* the adult world, on us and through us. We see with the eyes of the child, and at the same time we feel the child's gaze directed at us. This doubled intensity is an important part of Ibsen's power. The unblinking focus of the claim *against* us is reinforced by the sweeping assault on the elders and masters by whom we are limited and denied.

But the picture of childhood damage in *Little Eyolf* is a complex one. There is not one Eyolf in the play, but two. As a child Allmers's sister, Asta, was called Eyolf—in what itself may have been another scenario of abuse involving Allmers. Here, however, it becomes important not simply to summarize the story but to catch the subtextual rhythm by which we become aware of the peculiar sexual history of Allmers and his sister. For this is a revelation that masks as an evasion.

The day after Eyolf's death, Asta and Allmers fall into a kind of reverie as she sews a mourning band on his arm.

ASTA: Now the left arm.
ALLMERS: That, too?
ASTA: Yes, it's customary.
ALLMERS: Well—then go ahead.

She moves closer and begins to sew.

ASTA: Hold your arm still. I don't want to prick you.
ALLMERS: (*half smiling*): It's like old times. (898–99)

Why does Ibsen—always sparing, always pointed in his gestural notations—introduce this piece of business? The answer is that it allows a reenactment, a kind of regression to the scenes of their early life together. Under the subtle permissiveness of sorrow, Allmers is able to reexplore an old intimacy. Suddenly we are watching a pair of isolated, devoted children, prematurely freed from parental supervision. Their story unfolds for us, with a physical accompaniment that brings the old emotions to life, "distracting" Allmers from his grief.

Poor, orphaned early, Alfred Allmers had to care for his little sister while he was still a student. She in turn, though eleven or twelve years his junior, looked after him, mended his clothes, shared his struggles and ambitions, was his constant companion. To share his life even further, she chose—or was persuaded—to take part in a curious masquerade:

ASTA: But then when you went to college— (*Smiles involuntarily*) Imagine, that you could be so childish.

ALLMERS: You think *I* was childish!

ASTA: Yes, it seems so to me, really, looking back on it. You were embarrassed you didn't have a brother. Only a sister.

ALLMERS: No, it was you. *You* were embarrassed.

ASTA: Oh yes, I was, a little bit maybe. And I guess I felt sorry for you—

ALLMERS: Yes, you must have. So you hunted up those old clothes I had as a boy—

ASTA: Those nice Sunday clothes, yes. You remember the blue blouse and the knee pants.

ALLMERS: (*his eyes lingering on her*): I remember so well
the way you dressed up and walked around in them.
ASTA: That was only when we were at home alone. (899–
900)

This piece of cross-dressing gained her the male name
that she would have had if she had been born a boy: Eyolf.

Thus half-way through the play we learn suddenly,
almost casually, the real significance of its title. At this
point we may begin to wonder just which damaged child
stands at the center of the drama.

The above dialogue itself masquerades as a comforting
reminiscence, but it is subtextually charged. This is clearly felt when Allmers and his sister come to the question of
the reasons for Asta's transvestite disguise. Allmers, the
long-blocked author of an unwritten treatise on *Human
Responsibility*, is eager to disclaim responsibility here.
Both are embarrassed. The memory releases—or provides
legitimate cover for—Asta's "involuntary" smile and
Allmers's lingering gaze. Their conversation traces a delicate interweaving of barely acknowledged contacts—
approaches, withdrawals, denials, excitations.

In a moment of passionate lovemaking with Rita, perhaps the only such moment in his life, Alfred has betrayed
the secret behind the name Eyolf—and now, pretending
to remember what he has never been able to forget, he
confesses this to Asta, who is shocked. So powerful is this
moment for them both that to escape it Allmers must
change the subject back to the child's death:

ASTA: Alfred, you've never told any of this to Rita, have you?

ALLMERS: Oh, I think I did tell her once.

ASTA: No, Alfred, how could you!

ALLMERS: Well, you know—a man tells his wife every-thing—nearly.

ASTA: Yes, I suppose so.

ALLMERS: (*as if waking with a start, strikes his forehead and jumps up*): Oh! that I can sit here and [forget Eyolf's death]— (900)

In one sense it is a moment of authenticity—this is not the only time in the play that Allmers will be tormented by the ease with which he can be distracted from his grief. But it is also a flight from embarrassing truth; he "remembers" Eyolf too conveniently and dramatically. What began as an evasion now must be evaded in turn.

At this point we may already guess something that will only be confirmed later in the act: that the moment the secret of Asta's transvestism was revealed was the very moment, ten years ago, when little Eyolf was crippled. Alfred surrendered the information to Rita as a kind of tribute in the afterglow of orgasm. But even in this dialogue between brother and sister there can be no doubt of its oblique sexual intensity.

Eyolf's accident, which has initially been associated with sexual guilt, a retribution for Allmers's surrender to Rita, now seems to punish an even more deeply concealed guilt over his relation with Asta. And the sexual implications of both revelations are complex. Asta's male disguise seems at once an avoidance and an indulgence of sexual desire. In the usual Ibsen configuration of two women, one passionate, the other sexually cool, Asta seems at first to play the latter role, especially in contrast to Rita, and her boyish disguise seems to cover her sexuality further. But of course it is also a sexual release, a game by means of which Alfred and his sister could disguise, indulge, and perhaps erotically heighten their attachment.

The attachment is itself both intense and regressive. Alfred's first sexual response to Rita was fear:

ALLMERS: I had no passionate feelings for you at the start.
RITA: What did you feel for me then?
ALLMERS: Terror [*Skrekk*]. (913, 507)[1]

And at his single moment of unencumbered sexual pleasure with Rita, Allmers felt compelled—or empowered—to yield up the secret of his relation with Asta—a propitiatory gift perhaps, or the price of admission. But it also suggests a desire both to relieve guilt and to share a private treasure.

Toward its end the play behaves as if its deepest secret were a simpler one: that Asta and Allmers were soulmates, but because they thought they were brother and sister they never told their love, and, tragically, Alfred married Rita, in part to provide for Asta. But, as is so often the case in Ibsen, this is really a piece of sentimental dramaturgy promoted not by the author but by the characters concerned. It constitutes a touching interpretation of their relationship, but what we actually see of their behavior reveals two sexually dysfunctional and potentially destructive people—sister now moving like brother into marriage with a partner whose passion she cannot return.

It is hard not to blame Alfred for his sister's fixation at an early stage of sexual development and to find something chilling in his passing her private name on to his child—and the secret of the name to his wife. For it is in the originally secret relation of the two Eyolfs that Rita's resentment of her son seems to have begun, and in this light Alfred's confession to Rita may represent less a token of love than revenge on her sexual power. It certainly cripples Eyolf in more ways than one.

Ibsen sketches Eyolf's neglect with his usual unsparing eye and lets us see how each of many separate blows takes its toll. Filled with his new ideas for educating Eyolf, Allmers tells him, "Go down to the shore [and play] with the other boys" (873). The careless cruelty is breathtaking. Later, while Allmers is tenderly absorbed with Asta, "*Eyolf slips out unnoticed*" (878) to his death. Eyolf is and always has been a pawn in a slippery sexual game played by the three adults responsible for his upbringing.

We watch these maneuvers from a combination of intensely charged positions. The story of Asta, Allmers, and Eyolf may reflect the fantasies of an injured child, but, even more powerfully, those of an author who can fantasize simultaneously as both father and child. Here, in the condensed and overdetermined imagery of a dream, one can see the dynamics of a terrible battle between generations and between the sexes. Threatened by the power of

the mother's sexuality, the father displaces his feared cas-
tration onto the child. The child in turn fantasizes himself
as his father's true love object, a forbidden "sister," who
bears the child's own name and dresses in male clothing.
Thus he makes his father desire him rather than his mother, punishes/possesses the mother by replacing her, and
then punishes the father by rejecting his overtures.

This is important to us not as it may chart Ibsen's own
possible fantasies[2] but for the way the play makes fantasy
material available to us. We watch as if we were Eyolf and
Allmers, Rita and Asta, but we also watch from a mix of positions drawn from our own childhood dramas. The energy of the child's revenge, of the sibling's resentment and the
parent's guilt, of familiar rages and identifications both felt
and feared spreads through us to affect all the sexual link-
ings in the drama. It is a further example of an Ibsen play's
killer instinct, a channeling and heightening of our own ag-
gressions and fantasies which spring back, cruelly, on us.

Once again it is useful to return to a vivid moment and
explore how it projects a performance life. I have in mind
a passage late in the play that involves a difficult subtextual challenge for the main actor:

RITA: Didn't you use to call her Eyolf? It seems to me you
    confessed that once—in a private moment. (*Coming
    closer*) Do you remember it, Alfred—that wildly beau-
    tiful hour?
ALLMERS: (*recoiling, as if in dread*): I remember nothing! I
    won't remember! (914)

Allmers here seems haunted, not as Ibsen's fearfully crouching characters usually are, by emptiness, but by a fullness he seeks to deny. And for the actor here, the key question is what he seeks to empty out: what is it that Allmers refuses to remember?

To begin with, he is recoiling from the memory of the intensity of the sexual event, from the sensations of "that wildly beautiful hour." But he is also trying *not* to remember his betrayal of Asta, along with the suppressed sexual content of that relation. Of course he recoils, too, from the memory of Eyolf's accident and his part in it, another betrayal. And the memory of his pleasure with Rita must be intensely distasteful because he now finds her unattractive.

So that tremendous moment of pleasure, release, and shame gnaws at him even as he seeks to deny it. Once more, remembering and forgetting paradoxically entwine. The moment of disclosure, when he most fully acknowledged his relation with Asta, a relation he had otherwise tried always to domesticate or deny, was also a moment of infidelity to both Eyolfs. As such, it can neither be confronted nor erased. The wildly beautiful hour with Rita thus becomes a paradigm of the kind of alienated memory that Ibsen made the cornerstone of modern acting. It affects Allmers's every feeling and action, and yet its full content must remain always just beyond his awareness and control. It is the point in his past toward which run all the motifs of evasion in his life, the desires and deceptions he has kept from himself. It is the navel of his dream. We do not laugh at Allmers here, nor do we simply share his anguish. We feel the play's accusatory vise closing on him.

II

Little Eyolf articulates a connection between child abuse, sexuality, and history that is central to Ibsen's vision. Has Allmers sexually maimed his sister and then memorialized that abuse in his child? If so, he has maimed himself and his wife as well, for it is no accident that the disfigured boy becomes Allmers's final block to sexual fulfillment and gives him a weapon to punish Rita for her sexual energy, indeed for the wealth he has received from her.

Rita's wealth gives the play its social dimension. Her fortune has enabled Eyolf to lord it high above the other children in the play, who are damaged by poverty and beaten by their parents. Indeed the cries by which we first learn of Eyolf's suicide are the children's cries, initially mistaken for the noisy quarrels which reproduce their fathers' violence toward them. This makes for an extraordinary effect. For it is as if the sexual tension between the two wealthy landlord-parents becomes, first, the wild cries of the oppressed children and then the news of Eyolf's death.

The effect is modeled on the kind of climax we have already seen in *Ghosts* and *The Master Builder*. In what amounts to a grotesque parody of the new use of subtext, suppressed tensions seem to break out in large-scale choric eruptions. The climax to the first act of *Little Eyolf* is worth examining in detail.

A terrible argument between Allmers and Rita has been interrupted as Asta and her devoted suitor, the uncomplicated road builder Borghejm, come in from the garden. But the awful half-articulated threats that Allmers's sexual coldness has drawn from his wife ("I'm almost tempted to wish . . ." "Rita! I beg you . . . don't be tempted into anything evil") hang in the air as they enter:

RITA: I'll bet it's the evil eye that's played tricks on you here.
BORGHEJM: The evil eye?
RITA: Yes.
BORGHEJM: You believe in the evil eye, Mrs. Allmers?
RITA: Yes, I've begun to believe in the evil eye recently.
    Mainly in the evil eye of a child.
ALLMERS: (*shocked, in a whisper*): Rita—how can you—!
RITA: (*huskily*): If I'm vile and evil, Alfred, it's *your* doing.

Confused shouts and cries are heard from far off, down by the water.

BORGHEJM: (*going to the doorway*): What's the excitement—?
RITA: Look, all those people running out on the pier.
ALLMERS: What *is* this? . . .
BORGHEJM: Hey, you boys down there! What's going on?

Several answering voices can be heard, mingled and indistinct.

RITA: What do they say?
BORGHEJM: They say, there's a child that's drowned. (893)

Propelled by the misery of her marriage with Allmers, Rita's hatred of Eyolf seems to break the confines of realism and explode outward in the cries from below that announce, and thus seem to precipitate, the death of her son.

The same loud voices are heard again in act 3 as Rita and Allmers contemplate the "waste and emptiness" of their life together:

A raucous clamor of angry, heated voices is heard rising from far below. ALLMERS *goes to the railing. (932)*

Thus, even more than in *Ghosts*, we have a scenic orchestration that fuses intense impressions of inner and outer violence, of individual psychology and social dialectic.

The accumulated impact of such associations intensifies in the play's final pages. Like many of Ibsen's late plays, *Little Eyolf* closes with a kind of fantasy version of the modern social project, in this case the children's home Alfred and Rita hope to create in memory of their dead son. Class warfare, at least in their minds, is another possible cause of Eyolf's death; the poor children refused to save him, Allmers asserts, because they hated him. Now the warfare will be assuaged by a program of education, love, and generous subvention. But Ibsen has forced us to see an ironic underside to this project, to question both its motives and chances for success—just as he does with Løvborg's history of the future or Borkman's ode to capital or Solness's middle-class housing or indeed that early bitter parody of social melioration, the Captain Alving orphanage, later replaced by a whorehouse/home for sailors.

Each of these optimistic enterprises is inextricably

bound up with the tainted and ambiguous individual desires that have helped generate it. We feel them as products of evasion and self-delusion, as well as of oblique and thwarted sexual impulses. The liberal movement toward liberty and enlightenment is glimpsed as the enactment of a corrupt and damaging fantasy, often—particularly in the case of *Little Eyolf*—with its origins in childhood.

So *Little Eyolf* ends with the promise of another large-scale social project: comprehensive, progressive, optimistic in its outlines but tainted at its root. Like the Alving orphanage or the pedant Tesman's attempt to reconstruct Løvborg's vision of the future, the children's home Allmers and Rita promise to create has a dubious likelihood of success, since the talents and desires of its founders are so unsuited to what they intend.

To the extent that social optimism draws its political energy from the glow of good feeling it arouses, the dramatic pattern just described is highly disturbing. For it locates the source of this glow in the play of destructive impulses. Allmers and Rita hope to dedicate themselves to social compassion. But their desire is clearly a product of their guilt and rage, a response to injuries both suffered and inflicted.

The children's home that they contemplate takes its place as the last in a series of disturbing substitutions. The children are substituted for little Eyolf who was substituted for Asta who substituted for a boy and was fathered by the man who replaced Allmers's father in his mother's bed. And there are similar substitutions in Allmers's intellectual life—philosophy, the mountains, the "infinite"—all lofty, remote, high-minded objects of concern that help him keep what torments him at a distance.

The most powerful figure for the threat Allmers seems to spend his life evading is the Rat-Wife, "the old woman with a dog in the bag" who visits the house in act 1 and so fascinates and repels the crippled child. She offers to get rid of "anything here that nibbles and gnaws"(878); Eyolf follows her out of the house and to his death. Clearly the threat takes various forms in the play, and their overlapping suggests they are related: the sexual threat embodied in Rita, death, guilt, money, class hatred. Against all of them, Allmers marshals an ineffectual rhetoric of denial and transcendence—the law of change, the stillness of the mountains, the life work on "responsibility," social melioration.

III

The dramatic coherence of these many modes of threat and evasion emerges more clearly if we try to think of a spine for the play. *To get rid of what gnaws at you by forcing a path outside* works well.

In *Little Eyolf* the path outside takes many forms, both social and psychological. The children's home is a last desperate destination, but there are many literal paths, from Borghejm's roads to Alfred's errant journey among the northern mountains to the route Eyolf takes out of his parents' house, ending at the bottom of the fjord. "Outside" is also the path of exogamy, which has led Alfred to Rita before the play begins and which Asta takes to

Borghejm as it ends—the path by which these false sib-lings attempt, disastrously, to escape the sexual ties that first developed between an impoverished student and his preadolescent sister. From this perspective, social projects in Ibsen, from Helene Alving to John Gabriel Borkman, are always attempts to force a path outside, best under-stood in terms of what gnaws at the projector.[3]

This is indeed a complex vision, but its unitary force is perhaps best appreciated if we think of it quite literally *as* a vision, an achieved intensity of seeing in the theater, for which Eyolf's staring eyes offer a powerful emblem. And indeed, the final moments of the play present a crucial problem that can only be solved by thinking of drama as seeing. To understand the conclusion of *Little Eyolf* one must grasp the peculiar texture of the theatrical mo-ment—a texture that can be best expressed in terms of the *pressure of seeing* exacted by the scene.

In a sense, all final moments in drama invite us to take a long last look. Even a quick blackout only sharpens the afterimage. The end of a play inevitably reminds us of the special status of the theater as a *theatron* or seeing-place; we feel the peculiar attentiveness of our own gaze with un-usual sharpness as we are about to break it off. Some plays, however, seem to heighten the intensity of our stare, to make us dwell on what we are seeing. The stop-action finales of Beckett and Chekhov, for example, underline a frozen image. Similarly Shakespearean tragedy draws our attention to what we see at the end—Hamlet borne off by four captains, the heavy loading of Desdemona's bed.

Ibsen, however, is unusual in the extent to which he not only invites a long look as the final curtain approaches but makes us aware that we *are* looking and also aware of the shifts and edges that enter into our perception as we watch. We are not so much gathered up into the pathos or the visual or formal sensuousness of the scene as into the sensation of what it means to look at it.

Typically in Ibsen, though we may be aware of processes going on "outside," beyond the confines of the stage or the moment, we are nevertheless sharply flung back into the enclosed set and asked to stare. Morning sunlight gleams on the distant glaciers at the end of *Ghosts*, and we take in the chilling implications of that view, which stresses the unending horror of Mrs. Alving's dilemma rather than the question of how she may ultimately resolve it. Rebecca and Rosmer go off to commit suicide at the end of *Rosmersholm*, but the final moments consist of Mrs. Helsing watching them with a mixture of repulsion and fascination. Even in *A Doll's House*, though the energy that carries Nora out the door does draw our minds out to the (cold and dark) world beyond Helmer's cozy home, Ibsen forces us to look back at the onstage scene, to see that home as a trap, with Helmer now locked in it, an "empty" scene, as he calls it. The outer door does not open; it slams shut. By refusing us a path outside, these endings force us to contemplate what gnaws at the characters.

Not all Ibsen endings are like this. *Hedda Gabler*, for instance, seems to focus us not on the scene onstage, with its multiple centers of activity, but on the career of its heroine. Still, the effect is not so different from what we feel at the end of *A Doll's House*. The interior, apparently full of busy human projects, contains a growing emptiness. (Peter Zadek's 1977 production brilliantly brought this out by heightening the quotidian bustle on the vast stage space of the Tesmans' grandiose parlor. Brack, Thea, and Tesman were so cozily absorbed in their activities, it took them some time to notice that a shot had been fired in the next room.) In any case, the more common effect in Ibsen is the one that quite directly underlines the long look—and the point is again the special steadiness and savagery, the eye-opening implacability of the stare.[4]

How is the final moment of *Little Eyolf* to be staged? Rita reaches out her hand to her husband, and says, "Thanks." The flag has been raised, they speak of raising their eyes "upward," but their gaze remains level, as the stage directions make clear. They have agreed to take on the task of caring for the poor, abused children on the beach, but in a context which reminds us that this is a desperate move to fill the emptiness in their lives.[5]

The emptiness in this final scene rises, of course, from the terrible experience of loss Allmers and Rita have undergone, but it also seems to flow from Allmers's experience in the mountains, which he describes early in the first act and now returns to at the end. Structurally, what Allmers has discovered in the mountains seems to operate like a secret in a well-made play; it emerges in pieces, contested, guessed at, and worried over by the central characters—or rather it *seems* to be emerging. Unlike its well-made counterpart, the ultimate "meaning" of Allmers's journey—if it has one—is never clearly revealed. The imagery of that journey, however, is powerfully present in the closing moments of the play.

Throughout Ibsen's career, the high waste lands of Norway provided him with a complex symbol, varying somewhat in meaning over the years but almost always carrying a core of anguish about the potentials of human aspiration and artistic achievement. The *vidde* is a place where the artist can stand alone, looking down with a detached aestheticism on the ordinary scene of human desire and suffering. In Ibsen's long poem, "On the Vidde," the artist on the heights watches his mother's house burn down, concerned only with how the scene might be framed and rendered.[6]

The *vidde* is a place of emptiness and isolation; it is also a place of stillness/silence. And evocations of both *tomhet* and *stillhet*—terms crucial in Ibsen's lexicon—echo through *Little Eyolf*'s final scene. "Tomt" (*empty*), as we have seen, is Ibsen's most frequent marker of existential fear and isolation. "Stillhet" carries an ambiguous though equally anxious charge. It can describe the peace, the freedom from sexual agitation that Rebecca West attributes to the effect on her of the spirit of Rosmersholm; but for her it is also a source of radical sexual inhibition. Immediately after describing the stillness she has found at Rosmersholm, she concludes that the Rosmer way of life "kills happiness" (575).

So just as the remoteness of the mountains can imply a

callousness or suppression of affect that the idea of artistic detachment fails to disguise, so their stillness can also imply human inadequacy. Is the stillness Rebecca finds at Rosmersholm a good thing? It seems a surrender to Rosmer's own suspect desexualization. And the stillness of the *vidde* certainly fits in all too neatly with Allmers's eagerness to stake out a rationale for escaping the sexual demands of his passionate wife. Allmers has claimed to find some transcendent value in the "stillhet" of the mountains in which he got lost, though Rita has wondered if he was not simply scared by his experience. In the last act, though, with Allmers having acknowledged his bitterness and sense of inadequacy, the *øde og tomhet* (waste and emptiness) of his life, one feels in his concluding evocation of the traditional counters of transcendence a clear sense of *their* emptiness, their unresponsiveness:

RITA: Where should we look, Alfred? . . .
ALLMERS: Upward—toward the mountain peaks. Toward
  the stars. And toward that great silence (*stillhet*).
RITA: (*extending her hand to his*): Thank you! (935–36,
518)

Of course they do *not* look upward as they speak these lines, the last of the play. They stare, as Eyolf stared, as we in the audience stare, straight ahead.

I have been talking about the scene as something to be seen. And certainly all the features of the stage picture are important. But the intensity of the image here depends less on the specific visual configuration than on the intensity of the acting. There is a need for absolute honesty in performance, which is the vehicle by which the pressure of Eyolf's eyes can be felt by us as we watch the scene.

In part because of its technical simplicity, this is perhaps the most ruthless of Ibsen's finales, and as such it brings out much that is typical of his dramatic power. What do we see? We see ourselves, unsparingly, not to say vengefully revealed. We watch the tragic triviality of two normally selfish, greedy, weak, abnormally *insistent* human beings caught in a moment of more consciousness than they can stand. (The play is not only about discovering the unbearable, as so many of Ibsen's plays are, but about living with it.) Their tenderest, most socially positive affirmations are deeply tainted, their lives are built on a foundation of abuse. Alfred may be telling the truth, may at least be trying to tell the truth, indeed is insisting on the truth, but he can only use his old language of lies. Somewhere, far to the North, the confident young engineer, Borghejm, will be blasting roads through the stillness of the mountains, but at his side will be a pretty, recessive wife who does not love him, permanently scarred by her older brother's sexual games and her own complicity in them. Here, Rita and Alfred's hands may at any moment touch, but Ibsen refuses to let us know if they ever do. That momentary physical comfort is denied us, along with all that such comfort might mean to our sense of Rita's desire for physical and mental satisfaction and of Allmers's desire to be free of sexual agitation and moral guilt—all that it might mean to the desire we share with them for lasting hope and stable signification and honest mutuality. The flag has been lifted hopefully high, but night is falling. This silent, protracted scene of nearly frozen motion, with "the great silence" invoked and darkness pouring onto the stage, looks forward, physically and metaphysically, to *Waiting for Godot*.[7] It is the subtlest of Ibsen's avalanches.

CHAPTER FIVE

Lykke *and* Tro: *The Dramaturgy of Pleasure*

LITTLE EYOLF BEGINS WITH A TYPE OF DRAMATIC EFFECT that has been surprisingly neglected by Ibsen criticism—undervalued when not completely ignored. Simply put, the effect is very pleasant. An audience watching the play's opening moments can scarcely help responding to the many agreeable sensations on offer. John Northam is one of the few critics even to describe the scene in detail, and he catches its quality admirably:

Few of Ibsen's plays open with a scene of such opulence. We see a pretty, richly furnished room with plants and flowers in it; there is a wide view out over the fjord and of forest-clad slopes; the sun is warm, the sun of an early morning in summer; and Rita herself . . . is a pretty, voluptuous blonde of about thirty wearing a light-coloured dress. . . . She is unpacking her husband's walking-gear and chatting happily to Asta . . . about his welcome, early return.[1]

The appeal to the senses here is remarkable. A sense

of dawning, spacious physical satisfaction strikes us glowingly as the curtain rises. The green and gold of Rita's forests are being delivered at perfect temperature and in an elegant frame, attended by eager and beautiful women. This grand theatrical chord of fulfillment, experienced at a high, apparently healthy level of bourgeois comfort, rich but in no way oversophisticated, will perhaps remain in our recollection as a clear, if increasingly distant, alternative to the absences and waste places of the play. Other readings of this passage are of course possible. One could offer many accounts of the sensations solicited and their possible contribution to the play's overall design. But what is crucial for our purposes is the inescapable note of pleasure they strike.

All the elements mentioned in Northam's description are, of course, important for studying *Little Eyolf's* imagery and thematic development—as Northam, in a characteristically penetrating chapter, proceeds to do. But the immediate sensuous impact is also important. The role that this kind of pleasure—happiness, elation, physical delight—plays among Ibsen's dramatic effects has received little critical attention. And while it can scarcely be exhausted in a chapter, an approach to it needs to be attempted here, if only as a supplement to the kind of effect emphasized elsewhere in this study.

No topic is more commonplace in Ibsen criticism than *livsglede*, the joy or pleasure of life. Yet curiously the motif of pleasure opens a perspective on performance and meaning in Ibsen that remains largely unexplored—especially when we think of dramatic effect. Directors as well as critics could give much more thought to the ways in which pleasure and apprehensions of pleasure slip into and transform the felt texture of Ibsen's plays, particularly in the great realistic sequence.

I

To begin, one should note that *livsglede* is a compound, linking pleasure and life. This is suggestive because, in the poetics of modern drama, the word *life* takes on a precise, almost technical significance—both for Ibsen's dramaturgy and for the playwrights that follow him. Starting with Ibsen, the sensation of dramatic power, of artistic satisfaction in the theater, is associated programmatically with the sensation of life itself.

For more than a century now, innovative theater has represented itself, both to itself and its audiences, as a carrier of life. In the hands of an Ibsen, a Shaw, a Brecht, an Artaud, it has offered new kinds of theatrical experience with the explicit claim of reviving not only a moribund drama but a society perceived as dangerously enfeebled or numb. Taken as a loose metaphor, this program may seem nothing more than a cliché, typical of art in a revolutionary era. Far from being a vague slogan, however, this battle on behalf of "life" points precisely to a purpose that seems to underlie much of the technical innovation in modern drama and to the ways in which its greatest practitioners have shaped and altered contemporary consciousness.

The action of most, if not all great modern plays regularly defines itself as a struggle between vitality and deadness. Characters in modern drama are typically driven to act by a feeling of being cut off from the joy of life or indeed from life itself, a feeling that they are dead. We can recognize the motif in some of the most familiar passages in the modern repertory—in Ibsen's *livsglede* and *levende liv*, in the repeated concern of Chekhov's characters for the woods and orchards of Russia, in Shaw's vitalism, in the announcement of Pirandello's six characters, "We want to live!" The sense of an encroaching deadness and the haunting notion of a possible flowering is the theme that links Brecht's earliest heroes, Baal and Garga, to late ones like Azdak and Shen Te. And it makes itself felt in the great schools of performance style that have grown out of the needs of modern drama and in turn have done so much to shape its development. It is no accident that Stanislavsky begins the researches that lead to his system because he is suffering from a near breakdown, whose chief symptom is an overwhelming conviction of emotional and artistic deadness. The "method" originates in his attempt to recapture a creative vitality remembered from the past. Similarly, from Nietzsche to the Cambridge anthropologists to Artaud, the attempt, so influential on modern theater practice, to recover the origins of drama, reflects a desire to find signs of a now suppressed primitive vitality embedded in traditional dramatic forms.

The idea of life in this sense is one of the central and enduring motifs of modernism, in philosophy and social thought no less than the arts. It points toward pleasure, of course, but even more toward the idea of a lost *ground* of pleasure. Something radical must be done to restore the savor of an existence endangered by the circumstances of modern life. It is noteworthy that when de Man defines modernism in terms of a paradoxical mingling of remembering and forgetting, he bases his analysis on Nietzsche's discussion of what the philosopher calls "life." "Life," for Nietzsche, is that which breaks away from the past, which does not look back but lives forward from the present. It is a simple enough idea—that a regard for the past, for history, tradition, routine, study, works against our full alertness and action in the moment. But it suggests how peculiarly modern this intense investment of the idea of "life" is.

The modern sensibility tends to define itself in terms of a crucial agon: the struggle to overcome a broad secular awareness of social and psychological deadness. The deadness is linked to the conditions of contemporary life; modernism of whatever stamp is typically a revolutionary principle that will bring life out of the deadness, art out of tired convention, community out of alienation, lilacs out of the dead land.

This habit of thought also suggests the distinctive modernity of our own twentieth-century emphasis on theater as the art of the present, an art of presentness. For it is not only the competition of the movies or mechanical reproducibility in general that has made both theater artists and theorists stress the significance of theater as a "live" medium. The life of "live drama" depends on our relation, as an audience, to a living actor who manages to fill what we know is a scripted event with an impression of spontaneous feeling. This attempt to make what is belated, fixed, and determined seem present, spontaneous, and free is plainly of special relevance to the modern problematic of lost vitality and meaning. Theater, as the art of all arts in which pastness dissembles its own forgetting in the actor's pretended freedom from his script, is central to any attempt to capture an alienated or self-alienating real. So the deadness with which modern drama seems everywhere at war is at once the moribund theatrical past and the ever dissolving present moment of modern alienated consciousness, detached from God, from the hierarchical stability of tradition, from the results of its labor, from the hidden action of its primitive desires.

Thus there is an obvious connection between the sense of a large cultural struggle between vitality and deadness and the innovative formal or stylistic projects of modern drama. The motif clearly links the feeling for being alive to the feeling for theatrical technique; every important modern play attempts to revitalize a stage it thinks of as dead. Ibsen is a prime, arguably an originary example of this tendency. As we have seen, the call for life, so frequently heard in his plays, is also a call for a certain kind of theatrical life. The passages of life-altering fear that affect so many of his characters are intimately related to the demanding new histrionic techniques his drama requires. Conversely, the process of unleashing subtextual intensities among the actors in an Ibsen play is inseparable from his characters' struggle to escape from death-in-life, to be free of the ghosts that bar them from fulfillment.

The new theatrical experience of contact required and enabled by Ibsen's plays not only conveys but in large part constitutes their relation to life. This suggests why it is important to supplement what has already been said about contact and the *konsekvent* style with an emphasis on pleasure, pleasure not only as a drive in the plays but as a sensation. Moments and evocations of delight in the theater, especially physical delight, are likely to take on special force in a dramaturgy that presents itself as having a privileged link to questions of social, moral, and spiritual vitality.

I want now to explore some ways in which the awareness of pleasure in Ibsen gets mingled dramatically with the more negative apprehensions we have been tracking in earlier chapters. That Ibsen combines them, often dialectically, at the level of *idea*, is of course well known. I am concerned, however, with their presence as part of dramatic experience. Clearly it would be artificial to separate the sensations of pleasure in Ibsen from the many disturbing feelings—the many modes of fear, the excruciating constraint, the terrifying if exhilarating sense of what it is to *see* in dramatic terms. But a shift in emphasis will give us a fuller picture.

II

Of the many varied and frequently overlapping terms for pleasure in Ibsen, perhaps the best to focus on is *lykke*, usually defined as "happiness" or "joy," though it has a wide range of connotations. I choose *lykke* because it offers a particularly clear and typical introduction to the entire subject, and also because in several important instances it operates tellingly in combination with another complex word, *tro* (faith or belief), a relation Ibsen has sketched out in a famous, though also curiously underread poem.

In 1898 the playwright published a short untitled lyric, which he described as "the first preliminary work for *The Master Builder*":

They sat there, those two, in so snug a house
through autumn and winter days.
Then the house burnt. All lies in ruins.
Those two must rake in the ashes.

For down in the ashes a jewel is hidden,
a jewel that can never burn.
And if they search faithfully [*trofast*], it might perhaps
Be found by him or her.

But even if this fire-scarred pair ever do find
That precious fire-proof jewel—
She will never find her burnt faith (*tro*)—
He never his burnt happiness (*lykke*).[2]

The relevance of this poem to *The Master Builder*, and indeed to all the last plays, has long been noticed. It has in fact been treated as a kind of sound-bite version of Ibsen's themes—that is, as a not very surprising but eminently quotable formula. It is actually much more valuable as a clue to theatrical effect and process.

When one first reads the poem, *lykke* and *tro* may seem unremarkable, if not a little disappointing, the working out of the obvious implications of the startling imagery of the fire and the blighted marriage. Faith and Happiness are conventional attributes of the marriage bond; what else would one expect when lovers plight their troth? The poem may seem to go a little flat when *tro* and *lykke* come in. In fact the words reflect a dynamic central to Ibsen's dramaturgy, and they give this brilliant poem its final, tragic edge.

Generally it is clear that from early on the conflicting deep pressures in Ibsen's plays tend to collect around oppositions between faith and pleasure. The pleasure—sensual and emotional—that Nora in *A Doll's House* takes in her marriage depends on her belief in what her husband would do for her in a crisis, that is, on the meaning of the vows exchanged. After he fails her, one of the points they debate is whether *tro* is different for women and men. In *Ghosts* Mrs. Alving's vow to purge all traces of the Alving inheritance is seen as necessary to the joy of life. The play quite literally anticipates the imagery of the *Master Builder* poem. After the fire Osvald searches round the ruins of the orphanage, thinking of his lost joy, and Mrs. Alving searches for the son for whose sake she has made her vow. With *The Wild Duck* Ibsen begins a series of plays in which a climactic act of self-destruction issues from attempts to demonstrate a bond of faith. Once Hjalmar's pleasure in his marriage has been destroyed, Hedvig is called on to prove her love for her father in a way that will make him believe her. In *Rosmersholm*, Rosmer believes he has lost his capacity for happiness because he has lost faith in Rebecca West and in the love and admiration she professes for him. In the end Rebecca can restore Rosmer's faith in himself only by joining him in suicide, to which it is specified they both must go "gladly," a suicide, that is, whose validity as a proof of faith depends on its being a pleasurable act. Hedda Gabler demands a proof of faith from Løvborg, proof that he remains true to their old passional bond, and to prove it she tempts him to break his vow not to drink. Like Hedda, Hilda demands that Solness prove he is free and that he loves her, and that he deliver on the vow he made to her ten years ago. From *The Master Builder* on, all the later plays explore a marriage that has been reduced to ashes, where pleasure has dried up and faith has been destroyed.

Of course it would seem all too easy to assign a single summarizing binary to Ibsen's fondness for dialectical oppositions. Ibsen criticism has profited from many illuminating pairings of this kind, such as Shaw's realism/idealism, Lyons's (particularly suggestive) phenomenal reality/mythic transcendence, or Edvard Beyer's individual freedom/Christian transcendence.[3] I do not mean to suggest that *lykke* and *tro* subsume all other categories but they are an unusually flexible and suggestive pair, and Ibsen's poem indicates how richly suited they are to his thought. They also have the advantage of being simple words, at home in ordinary conversation, with all the slippery power of such words, the ease with which they touch the ambiguities, self-deceptions, and drives of common life.

Of special interest are the plays in which the words *lykke* and *tro* themselves figure prominently. The most explicit use of the dialectic is in *Rosmersholm* and *The Master Builder*, not surprisingly the plays that focus most explicitly on carriers of sexual stimulation, Hilda Wangel and Rebecca West. Revealingly, it is in *Rosmersholm*—written *before* Ibsen's "preliminary" poem—that the words occur most frequently (thirty-four uses of *tro* in its various forms and twelve of *lykke*).

Lykke and *tro* give us a map by which we can follow the flow of dramatic life in *Rosmersholm*, especially the central relation of the two protagonists. Rebecca West has not only awakened John Rosmer's passion, she has given him the courage to break with his past and his religion, to step forward as a liberal leader in a time of political crisis. Under attack from local conservatives, Rosmer begins to fear he has been manipulated and that Rebecca, who entered his household as companion to his late wife, the mentally unstable Beata, may have deliberately caused her death. Both come to feel crippled by guilt and self-doubt. Gradually, tortuously, they convince each other that only through suicide can they reestablish mutual trust.

From a director's point of view, the fate of any production of this play must turn on the dialogue leading up to their suicide. As with so much of Ibsen, the play depends on our sharing an inner dialogic movement of radical change.

This is not so much the play's meaning as it is its basic material. Just as Hedvig's suicide in *The Wild Duck* can be seen as flowing from the contacts established between Gregers and Hedvig in their series of dialogues, so Rosmer and Rebecca reach their decision as the result of a long series of exchanges whose currents are deeply buried and of whose depths they are but dimly and fearfully aware. If the change, the mutual persuasion to suicide, is not shared by the audience, the suicide has no meaning, because the material out of which meaning might be made does not exist. If in performance the dialogue that leads to suicide is not credible, the play fails absolutely.

Lykke and *tro* help us, as they will help actors and directors, to follow these currents in *Rosmersholm*. We can see this from the very beginning of the play, almost always a good place to spot the crucial dynamics of Ibsen's dramaturgy. His plays often begin with a distinctively subtle yet intense emotional charge. We feel tensions or strong energies which, though well below the surface, are full of a sparkling theatrical life because they are built up of so many details, as yet but glancingly visible though abundantly available to the actors. This charge is often invested in a woman, such as Helene Alving, who enters the play believing herself on the verge of a complex achievement, late (as she imagines) in a long struggle.

We first see Rebecca West in a position of apparent, yet curiously qualified control in the great house on which the curtain rises. This is Rosmersholm, the family seat of the Rosmers. Its atmosphere is clearly important in its re-

lation to Rebecca but is criss-crossed by conflicting energies. As in *Little Eyolf*, a number of immediately attractive
physical elements are evident:

*The living room at Rosmersholm, spacious, old-fashioned and
comfortable. Downstage right, against the wall, is a tiled heating
stove decorated with fresh-cut birch boughs and wild flowers. . . . In
the lefthand wall, a window, and downstage from this, a stand with
flowers and plants. . . . The window is open; likewise the doors to
the hall, and the front door to the house. Outside, an avenue of
huge, ancient trees is visible, leading out to the estate. The twilight
of a summer evening, after sundown.* (497)

The massed flowers, the evening light swim through an old
severe hall that has clearly not been designed to accommo-
date them. And out in that swimming light, to which all the
doors and windows have been thrown open, is something
the lady of the house (Is she owner, chatelaine, bride, visitor from far away?) is straining to see, to comprehend, to
guide. When Rosmer finally enters, having failed once more
to take the path across the bridge from which Beata jumped
to her death, his own charge—his own accumulation of
buried tensions—adds a further complexity of energy,
whose powerful counterpoint to Rebecca's sets this play
apart in the Ibsen canon. Out of his impulse to avoid, to
seek reassurance, to invite guidance, Rosmer initiates a
long, deadly negotiation over *lykke* and *tro*.

At every turn the prospects of *lykke* for Rosmer and

Rebecca hinge on varying crises of *tro*. *Tro* figures prominently in the maneuvers by which they push each other toward the death pact. For them there are always two important levels of meaning to the word: (1) belief in what either is saying; and (2) the ground of such belief— "You don't believe me?" "How *can* I believe you?" The answer is by killing yourself *gladelig*, that is, the act itself must be grounded in pleasure as the confidence is grounded in faith.

We noted earlier that Rosmer, in act 4, reaches a moment of terror when he cries out that he can no longer bear what he is feeling. Ibsen prepares us for this breakdown by a dialogue in which the prospect of pleasure is overwhelmed by doubt:

REBECCA: You don't believe (*tror*) me, John?

ROSMER: Oh, Rebecca—how *can* I wholly believe (*tro*) in you?

REBECCA: Oh, this murderous doubt—! . . .

ROSMER: Yes, it's appalling (*forferdelig*) . . . I no longer believe (*tror*) in any power of mine to transform people. I don't believe (*tror*) in myself any more . . . Give me my faith (*troen*) again! My faith (*troen*) in *you*, Rebecca! Faith (*troen*) in your love! Proof! I've got to have proof! (576–77, 323)[4]

Whatever tenderness and passion they feel, Rosmer and Rebecca are also killers at this moment, in the style of Kroll and Beata. The little hints, quickly taken back, like Kroll's in act 1, are devastating:

REBECCA: Take up the struggle again, John! If you really try—you'll see, you'll win. You'll ennoble souls by the hundreds—and thousands. But you must try!

ROSMER: Oh, Rebecca—when I no longer believe (*tror*) in my own life work?

REBECCA: But your work already has proved itself. You've ennobled one person at least—me, for as long as I live.

ROSMER: Yes—if I could only believe (*tro*) you.

REBECCA: . . . Isn't there anything, anything that would make you believe (*tro*) me?

ROSMER: (*starting, as if in dread* [*angst*]): Don't press this, Rebecca! That's enough! Let's not talk about it!

REBECCA: Oh, but it's just what we must talk about. Is there anything you know that could overcome your doubt? Because I don't know of anything at all . . .

ROSMER: Then would you show me, Rebecca—right now, tonight—if you—for my sake— (*Breaks off*). Oh, no, no, no! (581–82, 325)

But, sure enough, he asks her if she has the courage "to go the same way Beata went."

ROSMER: No! . . . You don't dare—what *she* dared.

REBECCA: But what if I had the courage? And I could dare it gladly (*Og den gladelige vilje*)? What then?

ROSMER: Then I'd have to trust (*tro*) in you. I'd recover my faith (*troen*) in my life work. Faith (*troen*) in my power to ennoble the human spirit. And faith (*troen*) in the capability of the human spirit to be ennobled. (582, 326)

Rosmer has seemed deeply hurt by the figure he has been forced to cut in front of Kroll and Rebecca and his former tutor Brendel, that of the whippable schoolboy, easily manipulated by others. Now he finds himself "against his will" shrewdly operating on Rebecca's newly confessed vulnerability. And he keeps tightening the screws:

ROSMER: I don't want to see you defeated. . . . You'll never be able to follow Beata. . . . You're not like Beata.

Rebecca replies in kind, with an equally lethal test of faith:

Come with me—and be my witness—
ROSMER: I said, I'll go with you.
REBECCA: Out to the bridge, yes. You never set foot on it, that I know.
ROSMER: You've noticed that?
REBECCA: (*in a sorrowful, broken voice*): Yes. I knew, then, that my love was hopeless. (583–84, 326)

For both the audience and the actors here, the question of belief raises the question of perception, of what it means to see. The characters' doubts trigger our own. What is the level of mutual confidence in this scene? How completely do Rebecca and Rosmer believe the interpretations they put forward? Is this a true renewal of vows impossible to sustain in any other way, or is it simply the detonation of an explosive mixture of guilt, shame, and fantasy?

ROSMER: We follow each other, Rebecca. I, you—and you, me.

REBECCA: It seems that way. (584)

Readers of Fjelde's translation may slide over the subtlety with which he registers the space for doubt (perhaps it is simply awe or fearful wonder) that creeps into Rebecca's last line, *Det tror jeg nesten også* (327), in which the shadow of a nuance about *tro* complicates the scenario of mutual desire. "I rather/almost/am inclined to believe that too."

And what are *we* to believe? What is it our pleasure to believe, what do we believe about their pleasure and the pleasure we take in it? Part of the torpedoing effect of *Rosmersholm* is that it puts these questions in play at the very end. For instance, do Rosmer and Rebecca actually commit suicide? We may be convinced that they do—certainly criticism has never doubted it—but the question of perception, of point of view, of seeing as a dramatic force, is vividly at issue in the play's final lines, which are usually underread. Commentary has treated Mrs. Helseth's concluding speech, in which she describes the lovers' last moments, in effect as literary rather than theatrical material, yet another piece of narrative that tells rather than enacts a story. Ibsen's main characters, the reasoning seems to go, are awkwardly unavailable to the audience, having left the stage in order to jump into the mill race, and so the playwright, creaking old duffer that he is, must bring on a supernumerary to tell us the rest of their story. And the assumption is that it is simply this by now very clear-cut story that we are being asked to follow. But if we examine Mrs. Helseth's speech with an attention to its theatrical possibilities, as a piece of performance in its own right, we get a passage whose effect comes not only from the events recounted but from her violent, rapidly changing responses to what she sees and imagines. Her monologue turns out to depend on an excited, shifting evocation of *lykke*, *tro*, and the emotions that war against them.

The first thing we register as we listen to Mrs. Helseth's speech is her gossipy prurience as she searches for the lovers. She is buying into the new salacious version of Rosmer's and Rebecca's life at Rosmersholm, the one now favored by Kroll and the local newspapers:

Out together, at this hour? Well, really—I must say—!

Next, as she peers out the window, a sudden fear grips her; she sees something unexpected:

Oh, sweet Jesus! Over there, the white—!

She quickly decides that what she is spying on is forbidden sex, and she watches with a scandalized fascination:

My Lord, it's them, both, on the bridge! God have mercy on the sinful creatures! Embracing each other like that!

Finally her absorption in sexual pleasure turns to terror:

(*Screams*) Oh! Falling—both of them! Into the water. Help! Help!

Equally absorbed, we are probably inclined to read the scene another way, as suicide. But it just may be that Mrs.

Helseth has seen it correctly. The lovers do not jump, they fall. Unbalanced by the sudden sexual release of their embrace, perhaps the first satisfactory sexual contact in Rosmer's life, they grow dizzy, like Solness, and lose their footing. We'll never know. Whatever the explanation, our only representative on stage at the moment, the *femme moyenne sensuelle* of nineteenth-century Norway, a faithful servant by her lights, with her narrow moralizing and hypocritical yet volatile, indeed eager response to pleasure, is reduced to terror. With her last words, she returns us to yet another character, another focus:

No. No help now—the dead wife—she's taken them. (585)

It is not the simple superstition of the white horses but the killer instinct of Beata (or is it Ibsen?) that has prevailed. Beata, too, according to her husband, had an overheated interest in sexual pleasure—though perhaps his was just underheated. In whatever form, their vow now exacts its price, and pleasure is punished. *Lykke* and *tro* together equals death.

III

Just as *tro* has many meanings in *Rosmersholm*, all mingling and reshaping one another at the most familiar and hence most radical of conversational levels, so *lykke* has a range of associations that spread and often conflict as the drama develops. The force of the dozen or so uses of the word in the play is much expanded by an array of related terms, most notably *gladelig* and *levende liv*.

Gladelig can have something of the range of associations of our own *gladly*, from cheerful willingness to intense joy, and Ibsen puts it under great pressure in *Rosmersholm*. *Gladelig* sets the stakes for the actors. At key moments, as when Rosmer and Rebecca go "gladly" to their death, repeating the word five times, it insists on a performance of convincingly pleasurable feeling against the grain of pain, sorrow, difficulty, confusion—against conflicting sensations that must also be rendered palpable and true. In such cases the actors must find a kind of courage or recklessness, an appetitive strength that can easily go flat or false if it is not sharply realized.

Admittedly, there is more than a hint of the ironic and perverse in the way *gladelig* operates. The eerily eccentric Brendel highlights this in his scene in act 4, which picks up the crisis of *tro*, the unbearable moment that rises to overwhelm Rosmer. In the manner already familiar to us from our discussions of nonrealistic climaxes in *The Master Builder*, *Ghosts*, and *Little Eyolf*, Brendel seems to materialize out of Rosmer's terror:

REBECCA: Proof? How can I give you proof—!
ROSMER: You must! I can't bear this desolation—this
    awful nothingness—this—this—

A sharp knock on the hall door . . . BRENDEL *comes in.* (577)

Brendel anticipates the imagery of Ibsen's *Master Builder* poem; he portrays himself as the survivor of a ruinous fire that has destroyed his home:

On this night what you see is a deposed monarch on the ash heap of his gutted [*brente*] palace. (578, 324)

And he uses *gladelig* in a grotesque sexual context:

[Rosmer will achieve his life work on condition] that the woman who loves him will gladly (*gladelig*) go out in the kitchen and lop off her delicate, pink-and-white little finger—*here*—right at the middle joint. Moreover, that the aforesaid loving lady, just as gladly (*gladelig*), cuts off her incomparably formed left ear. (579–80)

Anticipating Rebecca's suicide, he gives us a taste of the disturbing sensations to which pleasure can be linked.

Glad also glimmers out into another doubt-laden territory connected with sexuality in many Ibsen plays, one with an equally vexed relation to pleasure—the notion of stillness, calm, or tranquillity. We have felt its ironies already in discussing *Little Eyolf*. Rosmer seems at one point to link gladness to freedom from sexual perturbation:

ROSMER: I'll never again be able to relish the one thing that makes it so marvelously sweet to be alive . . . the calm joy of innocence [*den stille, glade skyldfrihet*] . . . A relationship . . . like ours—isn't it best adapted to a life that's quiet and serene [*en livsførelse i stille, lykke-*

lig fred—McFarlane translates, "life that's lived quiet-
ly, serenely, happily"]?[5] (544–45, 306)

And later Rebecca credits—and blames—the Rosmer way
of life with having replaced her overwhelming sensual
desires with *stillhet* (575, 322).

On the subject of stillness in this sense, of calm affection
free of sexual agitation as a superior alternative to turbulent
desire, I suspect Ibsen's own feelings were ambivalent.
Certainly he kept a careful rein on his own sexual activities
through most of his life, though permitting himself in his
sixties some carefully circumscribed, apparently chaste experiments with attractive young women, experiments that
may strike one as either poignantly tentative or cold-heart-
edly manipulative. But the advocates of *stillhet* in his plays
are often suspiciously undersexed or repressed, and the
cases they make often seem self-serving or self-deluding.
Ibsen himself may have been either of these. He may well
have been confused on the subject, but that doesn't mean
his plays are confused. Playwrights don't always get it right
or clear in their lives, nor do they need to—nor am I sure
whether on this particularly sore subject anyone can get it
right. The bundle of answers, theoretical, clinical, and
personal, that Freud, for one, leaves us with isn't particularly tidy.

But such ironic or negative associations don't tell the
whole story. While *gladelig* undoubtedly takes on a weight
of irony in *Rosmersholm*, and at times is made to suggest
sexual energy twisted toward self-mutilation, its positive

meanings deeply inflect the play. There is that breath of sensual fulfillment, of healthy joy, that connects with the flowers in the window at the beginning and with the passionate embrace that so startles Mrs. Helseth at the end. When Rosmer proposes marriage, Rebecca, though speechless a moment, cries out *i glede*. For decades the spontaneous pleasure of that cry has been overlooked by criticism in favor of the almost immediate suppression that follows. But for at least one instant Rebecca's joy is loud, physical, unrepressed. The pursuit of happiness in *Rosmersholm* is as intense, as promise-laden, as thrilling, even if at times as desperate, as in any play ever written. Actors ignore it at their peril.[6]

The sense of *lykke* and gladness in their full range of positive possibilities is felt most intensely in *levende liv*, a supremely elusive phrase. At one point Meyer translates it as "living life," McFarlane as "throbbing life"; when it next appears, both render it simply as "life." All these choices are quite justifiable, "living life" being the most literal. It is almost untranslatable in its near banality, the half-empti-ness that makes it so fillable by Rebecca's and Rosmer's complex urgencies, so well tuned to catch the history and the emotion with which they engage the whole network of *lykke-* and *gladelig-*words.

Fjelde renders *levende liv* very freely, as "the stream of life," brilliantly recapturing the intensity of the phrase in context, which any more literal English version seems to lose, by picking up the image of the mill race:

REBECCA: You wanted to plunge into the stream of life—
the living stream of the life of our time, you called it.
[*Du ville gripe inn i det levende liv,—i dagens levende
liv . . .*] (543, 305–6)

And a little later:

REBECCA: Because of that brain-sick fantasy, you'll turn
your back on the stream of life [*vil du slippe det levende liv*] you were just beginning to master. (544, 306)

Among other things, Fjelde's choice reminds us of the
richness of the mill race itself as an image in this play. It
suggests the painful vision of history as driven by psychology that runs through *Hedda Gabler*, *The Master
Builder*, and *Little Eyolf*. The mill race is both a natural
force pouring forth wildly beyond the dark confines of
Rosmersholm and a fatal presence haunting the characters with the threat of a vengeful past. Glimpsed above its
falls, shaken by we know not what combination of desire
and terror, Rebecca's shawl looks to Mrs. Helseth like the
white horses of Rosmer superstition. In human hands the
very stream of life converts readily to death.

But the large, liberating implications of this stream are
also felt, a sense of what is most brightly *living* in life.
Though the stream flows darkly and often poisonously, it
still glows with a possibility not only of individual but of
social redemption. We may sense this in the links between
lykke and *levende liv* that are spread throughout the text:

KROLL: When poor Beata put an end to her tortured, exhausted life, she did it so you could be happy—and

free to live [*leve lykkelig*] as you wished. (529, 298)

Through its force in the shared life of Rosmer and Rebecca, through the implications of what it would be to "*leve lykkelig*," we feel the idea of *life* taking on something like its full cultural urgency, its role in the large battle between vitality and deadness. It seems to expand to include the political, the social, the emotional in a single notion of conduct that can be both glad and free, responsible and true. To live a life that is truly alive Rosmer must master "the life of our time." And the life of our time cannot change unless it is lived *gladly*. For it is this word, so intimately associated with all the currents of their sensual life together, that Rosmer and Rebecca insistently apply to the new society Rosmer dreams of founding:

REBECCA: You wanted to go like a liberator from house to house, winning minds and wills to your vision and creating a new nobility—in wider and wider circles around you. Noblemen.

ROSMER: Happy [*glade*] noblemen.

REBECCA: Yes—happy [*glade*].

ROSMER: Because it's joy [*gleden*] that ennobles the mind, Rebecca.

REBECCA: But don't you think—suffering, too? Great sorrow?

ROSMER: Yes—if one can only get through it. (543, 306)

It is the combination of passion and suspicion, joy and doubt, that keeps the negotiations between Rosmer and

Rebecca so unstable and vibrant, but, especially where notions of pleasure are concerned, we miss a lot if we look only for irony. The thrust toward *lykke* and gladness is important. Their desire for each other, their desire to have pleasure, to be capable of pleasure, to overcome the blockage that makes pleasure impossible, keeps them shifting, attacking, touching, fleeing; it makes every moment between them *konsekvent*. Ghosts and gusts of fulfillment drive them on.

IV

We must return one last time to the little poem about *lykke*, *tro*, and the burned-down house:

But even if this fire-scarred pair ever do find
That precious fire-proof jewel—
She will never find her burnt faith—
He never his burnt happiness.

By now it is easy to see a further level of complexity in the poem. In the first two stanzas we have been led to expect that the poem's climax will lie in the couple's finding, or perhaps failing to find, the jewel for which they are searching in the ashes. But in the final stanza we learn that *even if they find the jewel* their search will fail.

Is there a higher object to the search? Once again, what is described not only looks forward to the last plays but reveals a pattern that turns up again and again in the realistic cycle. *To find the jewel* could work as a spine for many Ibsen plays—but only as an apparent spine. Characters regularly pursue what seems to be a superobjective, hidden and gleaming in the blasted, threatening scene—freedom from Krogstad's blackmail, the end of the Alving inheritance, "honesty" about the Ekdal marriage. But in the end, just at the moment this jewel is found, a deeper loss, an underlying blight emerges.

Ibsen's poem makes us reevaluate these plays, especially our tendency to view the characters' initial, illusory goals as trivial, superficial, the self-deceptions of people less modern than we. The figure of the jewel in the ashes suggests a different interpretation. True, one set of problems gives way to another that is deeper, more resonant, more recalcitrant. But it is a mistake to dismiss the earlier difficulties as mere deceptions. The two kinds of problem are connected, and the first set is deep and painful enough, and continues to exert its claims on the audience. Mrs. Alving's dream of a liberal, enlightened household, Rebecca's and Rosmer's vision of joining public and private happiness, remain valid; they are jewels for which twentieth-century audiences continue to search. And Ibsen's characters are usually still involved in the search as the play ends.

But by then their effort seems compromised at the root. After their knowledge, what forgiveness is possible for Rita and Alfred? Nora's dream of a true marriage can scarcely be distinguished from the emptiness her husband feels as the curtain falls. Under such conditions, to search for that which is *more precious than the jewel* is to enact one of the great nineteenth-century themes, one that emerges from the very process of the century. It echoes the search for Christian and non-Christian belief after the death of God. It is a search for what Matthew Arnold calls, "Joy whose grounds are true."[7] We search in the rubble for meaning and pleasure, but even if we seem to find them, how shall we recover their ground?

When Synge was an adolescent he had an experience typical of his generation, indeed of much of his century. He read Darwin and lost his faith. Significantly, he remembered the very instant of this discovery, or rather the more significant instant just after the discovery, when—having read indoors all morning—he rushed outside and saw "that the sky seemed to have lost its blue and the grass its green."[8] His entire relation to the world had changed. His loss of faith translated immediately into a loss not only of pleasure but of the ground of pleasure. It is again the connection between *lykke* and *tro*, in a form which captures the resonance that this dynamic possessed for Ibsen's age. To assert with Hopkins, for example, that "the world is charged with the grandeur of God," is to try to reestablish both *lykke* and *tro* simultaneously, revealingly enough through the insistence of an insistently innovative literary technique. Hopkins's modernity, the packed syncopation of his verse, springs from a need both to find new poetic life and to assert continuing religious faith. The excitement of his poetry reflects a desperate urgency. If the world, if the poetic line is *not* supercharged with grandeur, inscape becomes impossible; neither God nor beauty can exist.

Joy bears, in Ibsen, all its century-long accumulated weight of hope and doubt and fear. So that near the very end of his career, in the waning years of the century, even one of his most thoroughly defeated protagonists, one who among the final sequence of heroes is alone in being in no sense an artist, nonetheless offers up at a climactic moment, in a feverish, crazed hymn to capitalist ambition, an echo of every romantic ode to freedom and solidarity with the enslaved masses and the pleasure that comes with embracing them:

BORKMAN: That wind . . . comes to me like a greeting from captive spirits. I can sense them, the buried millions . . . You wanted your freedom then—and I tried to set you free. . . . I love you, you riches straining to be born! I love you, love you, love you! (1021)

"*Seid umschlungen, Millionen!*" Is there an echo/parody of Schiller here? After years of confinement, first in prison, then in bitter self-imposed exile at home, Borkman, the disgraced and bankrupt banker, has rushed out in the middle of the night. Stumbling ever higher in the snow, near death but "more and more exhilarated," he stretches his arms out toward a vast landscape—river, fjord, and mountain. What Borkman is addressing is capital itself—he tells us his first vision of the riches straining to be born came in a bank vault—but his language is one of romantic freedom and pleasure, an imperious effort to be free of buried restraints, a passionate sensual longing to embrace the captive millions. He dreams, as he has said just before this speech, of a "kingdom." We remember that Hilda in *The Master Builder* wants her kingdom and Peer Gynt at his moment of terror fears he has lost his. The key point is that in all these cases it is an inner kingdom.

One reason drama changes so radically in the nineteenth century—and why "life" is so important to it—is that it must adapt itself to the idea that the ultimate locus of action is now internal. The intense desire to "live"—or the inciting sense of being cut off from the joy of life—is an aspect of the romantic project of self-fulfillment. Like the feeling of being dead, the quest for self-fulfillment is hardly original with the romantic era, but certain terms of the quest become paramount as the era dawns, above all a particular notion of where fulfillment lies, of how the self defines itself and how the joy of life is recognized.

A major defining impulse of romanticism is the drive to conquer inner space, to possess internally a transcendent quality of being. This is often sought through action in the external world: revolt, travel, the pursuit of freedom; but the ultimate reference of such activity is internal. The quest is validated by an expansion, possession, or transfiguration of the self. Inner space is no romantic discovery, of course, but the shift of emphasis, the new notion of what the space is for, and perhaps of the effort required to explore it, is radical and seems to gain momentum as the romantic era approaches.

This must be contrasted with the search for pleasure and achievement as it is understood in earlier periods. A stress on the life within appears, for instance, in Elizabethan literature, but the relation between inner and outer realms is quite different; this applies to both the secular and religious perspectives. When Marlowe's Tamburlaine caps his great encomium to the restless human soul by defining its highest achievement as "the sweet fruition of an earthly crown," the phrase is apt to strike a modern reader oddly, as falling curiously short of the powers and ambitions evoked. We are likely to think of the sweet fruition of an artist or guru or philosopher as being greater because more inward, hence more profound. Tamburlaine's conclusion sounds odd to us because we no longer believe in the ultimate significance of outer kingdoms.

It is true, of course, that Tamburlaine's phrase might also have struck some members of the Elizabethan audience as deficient, but only because they would have been thinking of the *heavenly* crown which was the soul's true goal. For the Elizabethan, there could be no doubt that the splendor and activity of the individual's inner world only pointed to the glory of some outer kingdom, whether earthly or heavenly. Shakespeare's heroes venture deeply into the inner world and bring back news of the ripeness to be gained there, but, for even the most inward of them, that ripeness exists only in coordination with the outer world, usually the world of political achievement, in which the hero also lives in a primary way. Hamlet complains about having to set right the particularly ugly situation in Denmark; it is only romantic criticism that imagines him to be complaining about having to act at all. We are accustomed to finding the external world deprecated in traditional Christian literature, but this is always and only in favor of a better world, which is distinguishable from the merely internal world of the individual. The kingdom of God is within us, to be sure, but it is larger and other than we are. Only in our era do we find the outer world deprecated in all its forms, the kingdom of God itself but a metaphor for the properly self-delighted soul. And in this sense at least, our era begins with the romantics. Our concern with the joy of life or the unlived lines of the body or with finding our inner child (or with method acting) reflects a conviction that the most important actions take place not on the stage of the great world but in our hearts and minds—*i hjertets og hjernens hvelv*, as Ibsen says.

Even for Borkman, the sweet fruition of a capitalist crown is not that it is an earthly crown but that it is ultimately an internal one, in a way that Tamburlaine and even Marlowe could not understand. This *innerlichkeit* is the validating center of the entire modern project, starting with romanticism, and it shifts dramatic interest radically. Tamburlaine and Faustus look for ultimate validation outside themselves, restless and vivid as their inner lives may be. But Borkman, no less than Nora, looks for a relief and release, a gladness, a joy for which Schiller and Beethoven are simply an obvious expression.

Borkman calls his kingdom *uuttømmelige*, "inexhaustible" as Fjelde appropriately translates (1021, 562), but it is interesting that, taken literally, the word suggests "unemptyable." He looks for the opposite of the fear that has shaken all of Ibsen's heroes, fear of *tomhet*. This is why it is so important for performers of Ibsen to do justice to what promises or momentarily succeeds in filling up the emptiness, to Borkman's wild poetry and Fanny Wilton's bells,[9] to the flowers at Rosmersholm, to Nora and Helmer's powerful physical attraction, to Mrs. Alving's books and her continuing appreciation of Pastor Manders, to the dizzying mutual arousals of Hilda and Solness.

We should be careful to watch for such cues, for instance, even in a play like *Hedda Gabler*, whose heroine seems defined by her alienation from the joy of life. There, I suggest, something is to be found in the curious half-empty use of *skjønnhet* ("beauty"), so important to the play. Hedda has but the dimmest, vaguest notion of the beautiful, yet in crisis she insists on it. True, she asserts her interest in beauty merely in the way any shallow, provincially sophisticated, notionally racy general's daughter might; she is afraid to show her legs, uninterested in philosophy, politics, reading, even landscape. She has the worst blankness of her class to go with her affectations of superior sensibility. We can guess that her piano playing, of which she makes much, is not very good, likewise the product of a dreadful "aristocratic" upbringing—but even so, it is with a crash of music from "her" piano that she begins her desperate finale. In Hedda the inauthentic is so desperate, so hungry for inner space, that it becomes a kind of authenticity.

Jealous of Thea Elvsted's role in helping Løvborg complete his manuscript, Hedda burns it. When she gives the distraught Løvborg one of General Gabler's pistols, it is *beauty* she asks for from his suicide. The term is already a defensive substitute for pleasure, but for Hedda it is still intensely real, even in its vague way. Desire for *skjønnhet* lies behind the surprising phrase "vine leaves in his hair" which she invents to describe the heroic Løvborg of her imagination, the man who can return in glory from a night of drinking and kill himself "beautifully." For all its literariness, for all its ineptitude, for all its overquoted familiarity, "vine leaves in his hair" should not be underestimated. We must try to think of the effort it requires from Hedda's imagination. For her it is a kind of last-ditch sensual invention. Vine leaves suggest the Dionysiac, and the author of *Emperor and Galilean* would not have missed the connection to the god who as a child is destroyed by a jealous female and carefully pieced together again, like Løvborg's and Thea's "child" at the end of the play. Løvborg's manuscript is, of course, unlikely to have anything like a Dionysian rebirth, and the beauty, the pleasure Hedda wishes to assign to Løvborg glimmer only in the midst of her alienation from beauty and pleasure—in the crown she dimly imagines, which falls, as more or less literal crowns also fall, in *Emperor and Galilean* and *The Master Builder*, from heads too weak to wear them.

We must be alert to the vividness of such feelings and their dramatic force throughout the canon. When Maya, the young wife of the aging sculptor Rubek, goes off down the mountain with her lover at the end of *When We Dead Awaken*, her happy song is usually taken as a kind of ironic counterpoint to the ecstatic *liebestod* of Rubek and his former model Irene in the avalanche. Ironic, yes, but the effect is complex. Doubtlessly it represents a modest, bourgeois accommodation in the mode of George Tesman's kindly Aunt Julie in *Hedda Gabler* or Dr. Wangel, the understanding husband of *The Lady from the Sea*. Maya's "I am free, I am free" is a freedom of the valleys, of limited achievement and everyday sensuality. But her healthy appetite for pleasure is continuous with the vast and fatal urges of the sculptor and his model who, monumentally self-absorbed to the end, are also not without their ridiculous side. It is their foolishness as well as their grandeur that is supplemented by the song. *Free* is a many-leveled, self-torpedoing word, certainly, but it is also bodied forth in the happy voice of a young woman suddenly, sexually in love. And it is the play's last word—Ibsen's last word as a dramatist, as it turned out.

Ibsen and pleasure—the topic is not easily exhausted. A book on the subject could tell us much about the nineteenth century and our own. Here, enough has perhaps been said to offer an avenue for performers and readers who seek a more complete access to Ibsen's power. Summing up, one might say that of course the spectator should leave an Ibsen play feeling that the ark has been torpedoed, a shattering experience relieved by the exhilaration, the cool-eyed savagery of the project—but that something must always be added. The spectator should also be affected, though only barely and at best provisionally, by the haunting possibility of joy and freedom. It is only a possibility, but it is a possibility that is *felt*.

The drive for "life," for *livsglede* and *lykke*, like everything else in Ibsen, is a drive for contact, and we must not forget those instants when we feel contact is made. It is true that what is contacted is doubtful, deceptive, disabled, self-torpedoing, but the contact is there, if only in a cry or the sound of distant silver bells. And it projects a sentiment of being that is registered regularly both by Ibsen's century and our own: that to break through to life in this fashion, to achieve a vitality that has a sensual dimension, is not only a passional hunger but a kind of spiritual obligation.

This distinctly modern sense of a radical aesthetic obligation, of an ethical if not metaphysical call to pleasure and new life, offers a final clue to the role of pleasure among Ibsen's dramatic effects. In what is perhaps the most crystalline modern statement of the theme, this is the call Rilke hears as he gazes at the Archaic Torso of Apollo:

Wir kannten nicht sein unerhörtes Haupt,
darin die Augenäpfel reiften. Aber
sein Torso glüht noch wie ein Kandelaber . . .

Sonst stünde dieser Stein entstellt und kurz
. . . denn da ist keine Stelle,
die dich nicht sieht. Du musst dein Leben ändern.

[We have no idea what his fantastic (lit. "unheard of, shocking") head
was like, where the eyeballs were slowly swelling. But his body now is glowing like a gas lamp . . .

If there weren't light, this stone would look cut off
. . . for there is no place at all
that isn't looking at you. You must change your life.][10]

As in Ibsen, the work of art sees *you*. The poem vividly underlines the cultural meanings implicit in Ibsen's theatrical deployment of pleasure. In a way that seems emblematic both of the texture and the interpretive strategies of high modernist art, the poem pieces together an array of powerful apprehensions from a broken and incomplete source. In doing so it brings out the kind of radical hunger for revelation that underlies so much of modern hermeneutics—a hunger in which the sensual and the ethical are strangely mingled. Rilke anticipates the high modernist aesthetic model of the relation of fragmented, cryptic art objects to sensual fulfillment, which, as the poem helps to remind us, also resembles both the general psychoanalytical model of interpretation and the subtext/text relation of naturalistic drama. Like the modern notion of history as a science of hidden forces, all these models posit a texture of appearances that is gappy, deceptive, contradictory, incomplete, along with the obligation to find the hidden motif that will make these dead bones live. We have a sense here of human experience as a riddle whose answer is fulfillment, where absence is presence, where a fragment by a process of recuperation can make our bodies whole.

The body Rilke imagines is nominally that of Apollo but a tearing apart has made it Dionysian. True, Ibsen might find Rilke all too reminiscent here of his own Julian the Apostate, belatedly contemplating a vanished mind and a canceled sexuality, while dreaming vainly of a post-Christian resurrection. In the spirit of the *Master Builder* poem (and of the vicissitudes of Rubek's much revised statue, "Resurrection Day," in *When We Dead Awaken*), Ibsen might wish to add, "Even if you were to piece the lost statue together, the ground of its life would still be lost."[11] But my point is that Ibsen would also endorse the sensually conjured absent voice that says, "You must change your life." For this is one meaning his moments of pleasure carry.

It is like the familiar image of Ibsen reading the newspapers. Everyone knows how he would sit for hours poring over them. But what did he *see* when he read them? The image of Ibsen reading the papers cuts two ways. One is savagely ironic. The grand romantic ideas of fulfillment that haunt Ibsen's characters have their ineradicably shabby, suburban side. It is irresistible to think of the plays as headlines: "Tenure Candidate Shot in Brothel," "Local Builder Falls off Roof." But Ibsen also looks at the mingy headlines and sees something large. All these shabby stories, unmistakably *our* stories, vibrate to a crazy belief in joy. Unheard music accompanies the local builder's fall. Even in George Tesman's mangled reconstruction, the body of Dionysus struggles to rise.

If Maya's song must be given full value, we should be prepared to listen even more closely to the song that the arguably crazy Hilda hears in the air in *The Master Builder*.

HILDA: You don't hear singing in the air, either?

RAGNAR: It must be the wind in the treetops.

HILDA: I hear the singing—a tremendous music! (859)

The music constitutes an immense piece of what Stanislavsky would call emotional memory; that is, it is a vivid personal experience which, summoned in its full sensuous particularity, brings validating psychic life to the scripted moment. In Hilda's case it has almost the impact (and something of the sudden frightening certainty) of a reconstituted memory. Though she has recalled it, at least in outline, earlier in the act, and may never have entirely forgotten it, it returns only now with its original reality. It is a reexperienced event whose specificity and hallucinatory force would be obvious to a psychoanalyst. Hilda is hearing something remembered and forgotten, a memory of something that may never have happened that now escapes from the "past" and returns as a living fact, expected yet unexpected, a click, a confirmation. It is the singing she has only a few minutes earlier "remembered" having heard ten years before, when Solness climbed the tower, the prelude to the supreme moment when he kissed her. Now with "wild exultation" [*vill jubel og glede*][12] she hears it again (859, 482). She has also just learned that what she heard ten years ago was Solness declaring his freedom from God—the freedom that so frightened the nineteenth century—and announcing, too, the surge of vitality, of creativity that came with it:

SOLNESS: And when I stood right up at the very top, hanging the wreath, I said to Him: Hear me, Thou

Almighty! From this day on, I'll be a free creator—free in my own realm, as you are in yours.

HILDA: *That* was the singing I heard in the air! [*Det var sangen som jeg hørte gjennem luften!*] (854–55, 480)

For Hilda, what she hears has an overwhelming psychological reality, which must be projected in the theater. As Hilda remembers it—and as Solness has come to accept—it is a song of pleasure, of sexual and ethical consummation. In describing his moment of defiance atop the steeple in Lysanger, Solness has explicitly identified God with guilt, inhibition, the death of pleasure, fear of climbing where one has built. It is of some theatrical consequence that Ibsen has woven all this new material about the "singing" and its cause into the climaxes of *The Master Builder*'s final act, as if it were the revelation of some crucial, well-made secret. He makes it easy for the actors to focus our attention on the sensuous texture of Hilda's recollections, especially her lyric recognition and evocation of the music she has heard:

Det var sangen som jeg hørte gjennem luften!

The song in Hilda's case is a delusion, but it is palpably evoked. As I hear it, it is also one which much of the twentieth century has been devoted to silencing. It is the song of modern self-realization, beckoning us as individuals to the possibility of freedom and happiness on earth. It is seductive, dangerous, elusive, possibly mad. What it says is, "You must change your life."

ONE · TORPEDOING THE ARK

1. Richard Gilman, *The Making of Modern Drama* (New York, 1974), p. 46.

2. *Peer Gynt*, trans. Michael Meyer (New York, 1963), p. 123. Subsequent references to this play are included in the text.

3. All quotations from Ibsen in Norwegian are taken from *Ibsens Samlede Verker* in the three-volume Fakkel-Bok edition (Oslo: Gyldendal, 1962–68). Subsequent citations will be given in parentheses in the text. Except where indicated, the reference is to volume 3. When quotations appear in both English and Norwegian, the first reference is to the translation, the second to the original.

4. For the relation of *angstens alvor* to Kierkegaard's conception not only of dread but of despair, see Bruce G. Shapiro, *Divine Madness and the Absurd Paradox: Ibsen's Peer Gynt and the Philosophy of Kierkegaard* (New York, 1990), pp. 53–54, 127–29, 137–39.

5. Except where indicated, all references to Ibsen's prose plays are to Rolf Fjelde, *Ibsen: The Complete Major*

Prose Plays (New York, 1978) and will be given in parentheses in the text.

6. Francis Fergusson, *The Idea of a Theater* (Princeton, N.J., 1949), p. 150; Harold Clurman, "Notes for a Production of *Heartbreak House*," *Tulane Drama Review* 5 (March 1961): 60.

7. Cf. Theoharis C. Theoharis, *Ibsen's Drama: Right Action and Tragic Joy* (New York, 1996), pp. 277–80, on Hilda and Ragnar as representing two kinds of catharsis at this moment.

8. See William Worthen, *The Idea of the Actor* (Princeton, N.J., 1984), pp. 131–72.

9. Paul de Man, "Literary History and Literary Modernity," in *Blindness and Insight: Essays in the Rhetoric of Contemporary Criticism*, 2d ed. rev. (Minneapolis, 1983), pp. 142–65.

10. This aspect of modern subjectivity has been notably explored by Charles Taylor in *Sources of the Self: The Making of Modern Identity* (Cambridge, Mass., 1989).

11. Stephen Aaron, *Stage Fright: Its Role in Acting* (Chicago, 1986), p. 88.

12. Donald Kaplan, "Stage Fright," in *Clinical and Social Realities*, ed. Louise Kaplan (Northvale, N.J., 1995), pp. 389–423.

13. See Benjamin Wilson's well-known portrait. Cf. also G. C. Lichtenberg's description of Garrick in the ghost scene. Kalman A. Burnim, *David Garrick, Director* (Pittsburgh, 1961), pp. 96–97, 159–60.

14. Laurence Olivier, *Confessions of an Actor* (New York,

1984), 260 ff.

15. See Michael Goldman, "*Hamlet*: Entering the Text," *Theatre Journal* 44 (1992): 459–60.

16. *Selected Essays*, 3d ed. (London, 1951), p. 52.

TWO · ALIENATED SUBTEXT AND "REALISTIC" STYLE

1. Since the constraint appears particularly as an inner pressure that distributes tension and apprehension among the characters, it suggests anxiety in the psychoanalytic sense as well.

2. Peter Szondi, *Theory of the Modern Drama*, trans. Michael Hays (Minneapolis, 1987), pp. 12–18. Szondi is influenced, in turn, by Lukacs's similar view of Ibsen and the representation of time in the novel. See "Historical Novel and Historical Drama," in *The Historical Novel*, trans. Hannah and Stanley Mitchell (Boston, 1963).

3. William Worthen, *The Idea of the Actor* (Princeton, N.J., 1984), pp. 154–56.

4. Benjamin Bennett, *Theater as Problem: Modern Drama and Its Place in Literature* (Ithaca, N.Y., 1990), p. 22.

5. I may owe the word *contact* to Evert Sprinchorn, who uses it in a memorable passage from his excellent translation of Georg Brandes's "Inaugural Lecture" of 1871. In its published form, Brandes's essay was warmly welcomed by Ibsen at a time, halfway between *Peer Gynt* and *Pillars of Society*, when he was struggling toward his new style—welcomed even though Brandes had not entirely spared him in excoriating Scandinavian litera-

ture for its bloodlessness, idealism, and lack of reality. Sprinchorn translates *rent virkelighedsløse karakter* as "complete lack of contact with reality" (*The Theory of the Modern Stage*, ed. Eric Bentley [New York, 1992], p. 392). Brandes's Danish may be found in *Hovedstrømninger i det nittende Aarhundreds Literatur*, vol. 1 (Copenhagen, 1966), p. 23.

6. *The Oxford Ibsen*, ed. James Walter McFarlane, vol. 8 (Oxford, 1977), p. 343.

7. Francis Fergusson, *The Idea of a Theater* (Princeton, N.J., 1949), p. 156.

8. David Magarshack, *Chekhov: A Life* (New York, 1955), p. 383.

9. Fergusson, *The Idea of a Theater*, p. 153.

10. Joan Templeton is certainly and importantly right about the weird patriarchal hash that criticism has tended to make of this moment. See "Of This Time of *This* Place': Mrs. Alving's Ghosts and the Shape of the Tragedy," *PMLA* 101 (January 1986): 57–68. But the all too revealing oddity of much of the commentary she discusses may be traced to the deliberate oddness of the moment itself. It is meant, I think, not to be fully decidable or digestible as the play springs it on us— though it is also a rather wonderful, if desperate, mental leap on Mrs. Alving's part, a measure of the energy of her quest as it drives flounderingly toward "enlightenment."

11. Richard Gilman, *The Making of Modern Drama* (New York, 1974), p. 71.

12. Ibid.

13. Michael Meyer, *Henrik Ibsen. Plays: Three* (London, 1980), pp. 123–24.

14. Frederick and Lise-Lone Marker, *Ibsen's Lively Art: A Performance Study of the Major Plays* (Cambridge, 1989).

15. *Collected Letters, 1874–1897*, ed. Dan H. Lawrence (London, 1965), p. 240.

THREE · STYLE AS VISION: *THE WILD DUCK,* CHILD ABUSE, AND HISTORY

1. In *Time's Disinherited Children: Childhood, Regression and Sacrifice in the Plays of Henrik Ibsen* (Norwich, England, 1989), Robin Young is concerned with the immaturity of Ibsen's adults, the way they "sacrifice other people to preserve their own childish dreams and desires" (p. 210). Though his focus is very different from mine, a number of his discussions persuasively suggest the damage done in Ibsen's plays by childhood encounters with adult sexuality (see especially pp. 119–20, 132–36).

2. On the matter of undecidability, one further clue to Ibsen's continuing philosophical urgency may be found in a suggestive link between child abuse and poststructuralism. The issue of child abuse regularly raises the question, did it really happen? This is often considered an instance of the general problem of philosophical undecidability, of the gap between truth and representation. I would suggest, however, that the question of child abuse, indeed the very possibility of

child abuse, inevitably carries with it an element of undecidability—not because of the nature of reality but because of the reality of abuse. The problem is not, as it were, the general puzzle *did the tree fall in the forest?* but that child abuse specifically disables one from knowing whether trees fall. Child abuse is an assault on reality itself. Victims of child abuse typically lose their ability to distinguish between memory and fantasy. The result is a deep impairment of the child's sense of identity, a loss of the capacity to construct a self or to determine what is real (see Leonard Shengold, *Soul Murder: The Effects of Childhood Abuse and Deprivation* [New York, 1991], p. 16).

The mixture of doubt, rage, and imprisonment in fantasy, and the experience of this as a permanent condition—all characteristics of the mentality of the abused child—has in our day best been encapsulated in the "always already" of Derrida. This phrase, perhaps the most famous in the lexicon of deconstruction, implies an inevitable belatedness affecting all experience, a forced reliance on someone else's prior representation for all our information about reality. Shengold traces the origins of the phrase "soul murder" to a nineteenth-century study of Kaspar Hauser, the famous "wild child" from Nuremberg (17–19). "Always already" reminds me of Kaspar Hauser's phrase for his jailor and tormentor: "the man who was always there." Hauser was imprisoned, as it were, by belatedness itself.

The person who feels utterly cut off from reality

(and thus for whom the question "Did it really happen?" can never be decided) is in the position of this notoriously abused child. It is probably no accident that Hauser captured the European imagination at the dawn of the modern period—and that the term *soul murder*, now so common in the literature of child abuse, was coined to describe him.

Through these connections, both child abuse and deconstruction take their place in an easily neglected historical perspective—as parts of a long-developing anxiety that seems only to increase as our own century draws to its close. From Marx to Freud to Foucault, from the fantasies of schizophrenics to our familiar worries about the influence of advertising, a certain kind of apprehension keeps recurring. This is a feeling of belatedness, of being controlled from outside—a feeling that instead of thinking, one is *being thought*. It seems that there is no substantial reality to hold on to, either externally or internally, that we live not in a world of stones and trees and living air but in a prison house of words, other people's words.

Such anxiety and belatedness enjoy a curious status in academic culture today. Associated with lively and original methods of analysis, with new ways of producing new books and teaching old materials, they take on the very privilege which, by definition, they seek to undermine. They treat the impossibility of clarity and meaning as if it were clarity and meaning itself. For literary studies, in particular, arriving by way of writers like Derrida, Foucault, and Lacan, they carry the weight of disciplines imagined (especially by students of literature) to be weightier, more primary, even as they dissolve to paralyzing inadequacy the very notions of intellectual substance and primacy themselves. So what is, in fact, a mastering and destabilizing unease, a historically accelerating loss of confidence or savor, an oscillation of rage, indifference, and despair, becomes confused with a philosophical advantage, a place from which to lever the unfortunately vanishing world.

The analogy with symptoms of child abuse does much more than simply illuminate the uses and pitfalls of poststructuralism. It helps us to understand why we are so interested in child abuse and perhaps why Ibsen was, too. For him, as we shall see, child abuse intersects many strands—social, psychological, philosophical, political—of the difficulty we associate with modern consciousness and modern history.

3. The lines I have quoted are taken, in fact, from the earliest printed edition of Büchner's manuscript, prepared by Karl Emil Franzos and placed at the end of the text only by Alban Berg in the libretto for his opera. Franzos himself placed the scene next to last, concluding his version with an "Autopsy Room" scene that seems at best fragmentary in Büchner's original.

Büchner's manuscript exists in several versions, all incomplete and none authoritative. Questions not only of scene order but of transcription haunt the text. One alternative to the scene I have quoted, somewhat more favored by modern scholarship, distributes the motifs differently. Woyzeck, having murdered Marie, desperately promises his son a toy horse. The boy pulls away, and Woyzeck asks the Idiot who is tending him to buy him a "horsey." Again, no one is aware of Woyzeck's crime:

IDIOT: (*shouting joyously*) Hop! Hop! Hip-hop, horsey!
(*He runs off with the child*)

(Georg Büchner, *Complete Plays and Prose*,
trans. Carl Richard Mueller [New York, 1963], p. 137)

For our purposes the ambivalent juxtaposition of the child, the murder, and the terrible forces represented by the wooden horse is significant enough, whether it appears in Franzos in 1879 or Berg in 1922 or Büchner in 1837. But clearly Büchner invests his child with at least a similar pathos.

4. *The Collected Poems of W. B. Yeats* (New York, 1956), p. 214.

5. See also *The Oxford Ibsen*, vol. 5 (1961), p. 440.

6. See his letters to H. Schroeder and August Lindberg, ibid.

FOUR · EYOLF'S EYES: VISION AND VENGEANCE IN *LITTLE EYOLF*

1. Our sense of Allmers as inhibited and threatened by

sexuality is reinforced by what we learn of his promiscuous stepmother, who looms in his past like Gregers Werle's mother or Beata Rosmer.

2. Ibsen's biography suggests how he may have been empowered by his own multiple identifications in writing *Little Eyolf*. Certainly his lifelong bitterness against his parents, especially his father, reminds us of the vengeful child. Much of the inciting psychic material for the play seems, however, to have been drawn from his complex relation to his younger brother Nikolai. Six years Ibsen's junior, Nikolai had suffered permanent injury to his back when a maid dropped him. As a child, Ibsen liked to impress his neighbors with magic shows in which a mysterious voice issued from a large wooden box where—a fact never revealed to the audience—little Nikolai lay concealed. Not surprisingly, the collaboration seems to have been marked by tension and resentment; Nikolai threatened to expose the secret, and Ibsen kept him quiet by paying him off.

Nikolai's later life was unhappy. Never fully recovering from his injuries he became "abnormally shy and withdrawn," and after failing in business, he left Norway. His whereabouts remained unknown for nearly twenty years. Shortly before beginning work on *Little Eyolf*, Ibsen learned that Nikolai had died in America, alone and in poverty. He took pains to see that his brother's grave was cared for (see Halvdan Koht, *Life of Ibsen* [New York, 1971]; and Michael Meyer, *Ibsen: A Biography* [New York, 1971]).

So Ibsen must have identified not only with little Eyolf but with Eyolf's exploiter, who went on to adult success while the crippled child pined and died alone. The play, of course, is one last magic trick, both a final tribute to Nikolai and a final sacrifice of the child to his elder brother's career, itself a lifelong revenge on his family.

3. One measure of the cultural weight of *Little Eyolf* is that the spine *to get rid of what gnaws at you by forcing a path outside* itself dramatizes the general relation between text and subtext in naturalistic drama. Convincing naturalistic performance searches for a path outside, a visible expression that can externalize the flow of feeling hidden beneath the text. Moreover, this description situates the idea of subtext in what is perhaps the most general and compelling of modern hermeneutic contexts. Like the modern idea of history, it conforms to the pattern of a particular kind of secular interpretation that seeks a buried or dissembled energy deep beneath a deceptive, fragmentary, and troubled surface. It is the same hermeneutic habit we find in Marx, Freud, detective fiction, and *The Waste Land*. In this view the visible winding paths of personal or political history (or the flat and broken utterances of ordinary conversation or the apparently disjointed passages of a modernist poem or painting) are best understood as the oblique expressions of a hidden motive, a buried trauma or agony. In construing Eliot or Picasso or Joyce we find pleasure in

discovering the hidden dynamic. Freud and Marx (like Stanislavsky and Artaud) want the discovery to lead to action, to force a path, Rat-Wife–like, to relief from whatever leaves us unfulfilled or incomplete inside.

4. I say "stare" rather than "gaze," because the latter, in current critical usage, emphasizes the viewer as desiring subject, the owner or explorer of the scene. That is present in Ibsen, too, but more dominant is the stare, which seems to animate us from many psychic sources; it is more like having our eyes propped open with toothpicks, with being forced "above all to see."

5. In a powerful if controversial analysis, Naomi Lebowitz sees the *kindermord* motif in Ibsen more positively, as carrying a redemptive impulse—not as sacrifice (this would be the sentimental vision parodied in *The Wild Duck*) but as a cruel clearing of the moral ground, an opening up of the realm of spiritual possibility which she calls the Great World (see Lebowitz, *Ibsen and the Great World* [Baton Rouge, 1990], pp. 90–92).

6. The emphasis on detachment scarcely conceals yet another version of the child's revenge.

7. "Silence," Beckett said of *Godot*, "is pouring into this play like water into a sinking ship."

FIVE · *LYKKE* AND *TRO*: THE DRAMATURGY OF PLEASURE

1. John Northam, *Ibsen: A Critical Study* (Cambridge,

1973), p. 186.

2. I have slightly adapted McFarlane's translation in *The Oxford Ibsen*, vol. 7, p. 521.

3. Shaw, *The Quintessence of Ibsenism* (1891); Charles Lyons, *Henrik Ibsen: The Divided Consciousness* (Carbondale, Ill., 1972) ; Edvard Beyer, "Henrik Ibsens *Rosmersholm*," in *En Ny Ibsen? Ni Ibsen-Artikler*, ed. Harald Noreng (Oslo, 1979).

4. Here and in the next quotation I have made Fjelde's translation slightly more literal in places, in order to keep it consistent with the varying forms of *tro* that appear in Ibsen's text.

5. For McFarlane's translation see *The Oxford Ibsen*, vol. 6, p. 341.

6. Errol Durbach has a particularly interesting reading of Rebecca's rejection of Rosmer's proposal, which attributes it to her moral shock on hearing her own shout of joy:

> Motives stand revealed in such shocking clarity that, in her next breath, she immediately cancels all hope of freedom, joy, and passion by refusing her most ardently sought-after goal. . . . The impossibility of becoming Rosmer's wife in this world . . . has its basis, here, in the gradual redefinition of *joy* from the scream of amoral triumph to the act of ethical justice joyfully performed at the close of the play.
>
> (*"Ibsen the Romantic": Analogues of Paradise in the Later Plays* [Athens, Ga., 1982], p. 182)

My discussion leaves room for many readings, including Durbach's. But I am less impressed than he is by the characters' expressions of ethical high-mindedness at the end.

Durbach's view of the play insists on a sharp distinction between *glede* and *lykke*. "It is not 'joy,' not *glede*, that Rosmersholm destroys, but 'pleasure'" (ibid., p. 184). I think, however, that the continuities betweeen the two words are as important for Ibsen as their differences, and that the former have been rather neglected by criticism. Indeed I am inclined to say that although there are important nuances in Rosmersholm between sensual pleasure and a kind of philosophical joy, Ibsen's language reflects their complex blurring at least as much as it distinguishes them (cf. Rosmer's speeches, quoted above on p. 135, where sexual "stillness" is described as both *glade* and *lykkelig*. Durbach does, however, provide a penetrating account of the play's ethical tensions.

Future discussions of this scene will, I hope, also take note of Janet Garton's brilliant observation that Rebecca's ultimate rejection of Rosmer's proposal has much to do with his telltale formulation, "Will you be my *second* wife?" ("The Middle Plays," in *The Cambridge Companion to Ibsen*, ed. James McFarlane [Cambridge, 1994], pp. 111–12).

7. "Obermann Once More," l. 238.

8. David H. Greene and Edward M. Stephens, *J. M. Synge, 1871–1909*, rev. ed. (New York, 1989), p. 9.

9. The bells strike an unexpected note in the grim setting

on which the first act curtain of *John Gabriel Borkman* rises. They are the first sound we hear in the play; when she hears them, Gunhild's eyes light up with joy (*det tindrer av glede i hennes øyne*) (943, 521).

10. *Selected Poems of Rainer Maria Rilke*, trans. Robert Bly (New York, 1981), pp. 146–47.

11. For Rubek, life says, "You must change your statue." Irene, the model of the original statue, returns from the dead to tell him, "You must change your life because you have never lived" (1080).

12. Ibsen also uses *jubel* (exultation, jubilation, song of joy) to describe Maja's singing at the end of *When We Dead Awaken* (600).

3626